Lincoln College, Oxford

THE REV. W. W. MERRY, D.D., RECTOR

NCOLN COLLEGE OXFORD

BY

STEPHEN A. WARNER, B.A.

THE LINCOLN IMP

.

ᴸᴼ LONDON
SIDGWICK & JACKSON, LTD.
3 ADAM STREET, ADELPHI, W.C.

First Issued 1908

RECTORI SOCIISQUE
COLLEGII BEATAE MARIAE
ET OMNIUM SANCTORUM LINCOLN :
IN UNIVERSITATE OXON.

CONTENTS

CONTENTS

LIST OF ILLUSTRATIONS

LIST OF ILLUSTRATIONS

PREFACE

THIS book in no way pretends to be exhaustive as far as the history of Lincoln is concerned, for a fuller account of which readers are referred to the Rev. A. Clark's excellent work; but the author makes bold to say that there are very few objects of interest in the College which have not been here reproduced, for the first time, in some way or another.

He especially wishes to acknowledge the kindness of the Rev. Andrew Clark, LL.D., in helping with much information and many suggestions, and for his great generosity in allowing the author free access to his hitherto unpublished MS. notes on the College Account Books and other matters connected with Lincoln.

He also cordially thanks his Rector for kindly help and enthusiasm, for his snap-shot of "Beating the Bounds," and every facility for carrying through the work; his old College friend, Mr. Arnold Fairbairns, for his magnificent series of photographs for the collotype illustrations, which, owing to reduction, hardly do justice to the beauty of the originals; to Mr. Simmonds, the porter; Mr. Lewis, the maniple; and many others, of whom want of space forbids a mention by name.

The author feels that he owes much more to his helpers than he could have wished, but he has at least the pleasure of knowing that, with a very few exceptions, it is entirely the work of Lincoln men, including the verses at the end, written by Dr. James Williams, the "poet of the Oxford Mag."

S. A. W.

April 25, 1908

THANKSGIVING FOR PIOUS FOUNDERS AND BENEFACTORS

O LORD GOD, who art the Life and Resurrection of them that believe in Thee, as well to be praised for the dead as for the living; We give Thee humble thanks for our Founders, Richard Fleming, Bishop of Lincoln; and Thomas Rotheram, Archbishop of York; and all our other Benefactors: such as were Emily Carr, Widow; John Southam, Archdeacon of Oxford; John Forrest, Dean of Wells; William Finderne of Childrey, Esq.; Henry Beaufort, Cardinal and Bishop of Winchester; John Bucktot, Priest; Robert Fleming, Dean of Lincoln; Thomas Beckington, Bishop of Bath and Wells; William Dagville, Alderman of Oxford; John Crosby, Treasurer of Lincoln; Walter Bate, M.A.; William Smyth, Bishop of Lincoln; Sir William Finderne, Knt.; Margaret Parker, Widow; Edmund Audley, Bishop of Sarum; Edward Darby, Archdeacon of Stowe; Robert Trappes, Citizen of London, and Joan, his wife; Richard Kilby, Rector; John Randall, Fellow; Sir Thomas Rotheram, Knt.; Thomas Marshall, Rector and Dean of Gloucester; William Hopkins, Steward; Fitzherbert Adams, Rector; Sir John Thorold of Cranwell, Bart.; Nathaniel Lord Crewe, Rector and Bishop of Durham; John Morley, Rector; Richard Hutchins, Rector; Elizabeth Tatham, Widow; John Radford, Rector; Henry Usher Matthews, M.A.; Edward William Stillingfleet, Fellow; Edward Grinfield, M.A.; Thomas Fowler, D.D.; and all the rest of our Benefactors, by whose benefits we are here maintained to godliness and good learning; beseeching Thee, that, as, we trust, their souls live for ever with Thee in Heaven, so their blessed memory may never die with us on earth. Give us grace, O Lord, that we may use these their benefits to the honour, praise, and glory of Thy Holy Name, and to the good end and purpose whereunto they were bestowed upon us; and be finally brought with them to the glory of that immortal Resurrection; through Jesus Christ, our only Lord and Saviour. Amen.

We further praise Thee, O Lord, for Thy blessing vouchsafed to us in the munificence of the Right Reverend John Williams, Bishop of Lincoln, who built us this beautiful House, consecrated to Thy service: beseeching Thee to give us grace to make good use of the same in the performance of better service unto Thee in this place, to the honour of Thy Name, through our Lord and Saviour Jesus Christ. Amen.

INTRODUCTION

EARLY in the fifteenth century, on the spot where now is Lincoln College, there stood the Church of St. Mildred, surrounded by numerous "Halls," which served as homes for students in the University, then rapidly increasing. The parish of St. Mildred, squeezed in between the more important ones of All Saints and St. Michael, was very poor and circumscribed, and for this reason Richard Fleming, Bishop of Lincoln, no doubt thought that little harm would be done in pulling down a church no longer needed and taking the site for his proposed "collegiolum." His idea was to found a "little college," somewhat on the lines of the modern theological college, for graduates only who should there be brought up in the strict faith of the Church, and then go forth to combat the spreading doctrines of Wyclif.

In 1427 he obtained a charter from the King to unite the three parishes of All Saints, St. Michael, and St. Mildred into a collegiate church, with a College consisting of a Rector, seven Scholars, and two Chaplains to serve the Churches. His own foundation charter was given in 1429, appointing William Chamberleyn to be the first Rector of the "College of the Blessed Mary and All Saints, Lincoln," and steps were at once taken to demolish St. Mildred's and purchase the neighbouring Crauneford Hall and Deep Hall, on the site of which part of the east side and the south-west corner of the front quadrangle were built.

3

INTRODUCTION

Unfortunately Fleming died intestate in 1431, and Chamberleyn in 1434, before any great progress had been made; but the energy and enthusiasm of the second Rector, John Beke, saved the College from the extinction which threatened it. He obtained a "notable sum of money" from John Southam, Archdeacon of Oxford, with which he purchased the rest of the site for the front quadrangle and induced John Forrest, Dean of Wells, to erect the buildings then lacking. When the work was finished the College was composed of the Kitchen, the building connecting it with the Buttery, now the Manciple's Room and Guest Room, and the front "quad," with the exception of the southern side.

However, on the accession of Edward IV, in 1461, the College was in great danger of being suppressed. The King was in need of money, and it was suggested that such bodies as Lincoln College, which were considered illegally constituted as deriving their title from the deposed Henry VI, should be abolished and their property confiscated. The new Rector, John Tristropp, a worthy successor to Beke, appealed to George Nevill, Chancellor of the University and Lord High Chancellor of England, who, by his influence, induced the King to spare the College and "pardon all transgressions" up to November 4, 1461. Successful though this issue seemed to be, there yet lurked in the "form" of confirmation then granted a flaw which, a few years later, was the cause of a renewal of the old trouble. Whether by mistake or of set purpose the Royal Grant was made "to the Rector and scholars" only, whereas in the College draft the words had run "to the Rector, scholars, *and their successors.*" It is curious to note that in 1474, when the Nevill influence had waned, another attempt was made, on the strength of this important omission, to procure the abolition of the College on the ground that with the death of the existing members it would lapse to the Crown. This time the College appealed to its Visitor, Thomas Rotheram, Bishop of Lincoln; and the manner of the appeal, so well known to all Lincoln men, is graphically described (in 1558) by the Sub-Rector, Robert

4

Parkinson, in the College register. It was on the occasion when Rotheram was in Oxford, in the course of visiting his diocese, that the Rector, or one of the Fellows, preached before him upon the text taken from Psalm lxxx, "Behold, and visit this vine . . ." He drew so harrowing a picture of the poverty and distress of the College, and its present imminent danger of extinction, that the Bishop, touched by his story, promised that he would come to their aid. In 1478 he obtained another charter, whereby the College was to be a perpetual corporation, settled anew on a surer basis, and with a grant of further privileges. To this day a grateful remembrance of the man who was in very truth our second Founder keeps a vine growing in the chapel quadrangle. Loggan's view shows a vine also creeping up one of the buttresses of the Hall, and until 1900 there was another growing on the wall of the Guest Room. The former has, unfortunately, been replaced by a virginia creeper, while the latter died and had to be cut down. It is clear, too, that in former times this picturesque incident was not forgotten, for running through the old account books are continual items such as the following: (1529) "to Thos. Poole for cuttyng of the vyne"; (1650) "for nayles to nayle up the vine in the quadrangle" (probably Loggan's tree); (1670) "for pruning the vines in the quadrangle"; and (1764) "to the gardener for a grape tree, 9d." All these entries go to show that although these vines may not have been grown and tended solely as an act of commemoration, nevertheless, there was the remembrance underlying, and to-day they are essentially the memento of a striking event in College history.

To return to the buildings. In the year 1465 Thomas Beckington, Bishop of Bath and Wells, died, and his executors, out of money that he left for charitable purposes, gave £200, with which the present Rector's lodgings, adjoining the Hall in the south-east corner of the front quadrangle, were built. His arms and correct rebus (a beacon in a tun) are on the wall and buttress in the "Grove," those in the front and chapel

INTRODUCTION

quadrangles being comparatively modern. The remaining portion of the quadrangle was completed by Rotheram, as is shown by the stone angels on the wall holding shields which bear his arms.

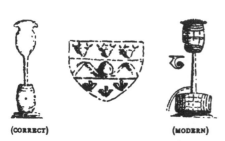

The sixty years which followed on the re-settlement of the College were years of generous benefactions. First and foremost comes the Dagville-Parker bequest. By his will, dated June 2, 1474, William Dagville, a rich citizen of Oxford, bequeathed his inn, called "Dagville's Inn" (known in 1341 as "Romyns Hall," then as "Croxford's Inn," and now as the "Mitre Hotel"), the "Christopher Inn" (now part of Messrs. Elliston and Cavell's premises), and a considerable amount of other property to his young wife for life, with a gift over of the "Mitre" to his daughter Joan, and of the "Christopher" to the Rector and Fellows of Lincoln College, "to kepe every yere my mynde," i.e., to keep the anniversary of his death. If Joan died without issue, then all the property was to come to the College. Margaret, Dagville's widow, married again, and in 1489, as Margaret Parker, widow, she leased the "Mitre" and the "Christopher" to the College, at a yearly rental of ten marcs. These two inns, with a garden, now occupied by the city market, were the only Dagville property which ultimately found its way to Lincoln. In 1508 William Smyth, Bishop of Lincoln, gave his manors of Senclers, in Chalgrove, Oxfordshire, and of Elston (or Bushbury), in Staffordshire, together containing about 520 acres, to the College unconditionally. He also contemplated further benefactions with regard to Fellowships for members of his native county of Lancashire and his former diocese of

Lichfield; but as the College would probably not agree to this alteration in the statutes, he devoted them instead to his new foundation of Brasenose. About the same date another benefactor appears in the person of Edmund Audley, Bishop of Salisbury. He gave a large number of books to the Library and £40 with which to buy lands and apply the rents "pro robis," i.e., to buy robes for the Fellows. In 1521 the money was "deliuered to Mr. Subrector for byyng of our leuoras" (i.e., liveries), and a sum of £2 is still paid annually to the Rector and Senior Fellows for this purpose. He also built a chantry chapel in his Cathedral, to be served by a priest chosen from the Fellows of Lincoln. An interesting entry in the account for the year 1517 runs: "For a payre of glouys (i.e., gloves) furryd with lettys (said to be the winter coat of the polecat) that Master Cottysford had to my lord of Salysbury, 2s." The fourth great benefactor was Edward Darby, Archdeacon of Stow, who was Fellow in 1495 and Senior Proctor five years later. He gave a considerable sum of money to the College in 1537, wherewith to buy lands in Yorkshire and endow three new Fellowships, one to be filled by a native of Oxfordshire, nominated by the Bishop of Lincoln, hence called the "bishop's fellow," the other two elected by the Rector and Fellows, one from Leicestershire or Northamptonshire, and one from the Archdeaconry of Stow.

During the Reformation Period, Lincoln stood out as a thoroughly Roman Catholic College. Its constitution, and even its buildings, had always been of a monastic character, its training, with the exception of a Canon Law Fellow, entirely theological, and its religious exercises largely taken up with the observance of the anniversaries of deaths of benefactors and persons who had left special sums for masses for their souls. At this time the account books show the College endeavouring to serve two masters: (1549) "for rysshes (i.e., rushes) for the hall, chappell, and lybrarie agaynst the Vysytors commynge" (i.e., Edward VI's Commissioners); and in the same year, "for syngynge breed (i.e., wafers for celebration) to the chapel, for wyne the tyme we had *masse*." A succession of Rectors, some open, some secret adherents of the old faith, kept the College to its former ways. In 1554, the Rector, Hugh Weston, Archdeacon of Colchester and Professor of Divinity, was made chairman of the Commission appointed to dispute with Cranmer, Latimer, and Ridley, prior to their execution. He was followed by Christopher Hargreaves, a famous Romanist champion, and his successor again, Henry Henshaw, was ejected in 1560 by Elizabeth's visitors. These last endeavoured to bring the colleges to a right way of thinking by pushing outsiders into the head-ships, contrary to the statutes, but, curiously enough, on the three successive occasions on which this was done at Lincoln the intruder in each case turned out to be of Romanist leanings. In one instance, Francis Babington (1560-63) became suspected, owing to a slip made in the funeral sermon which he, as Robert Dudley's Chaplain, had to preach over the unfortunate Amy Robsart, when, by mistake, he blurted out, "I recommend to your memories this virtuous lady so pitifully *murdered*." In another case, John Bridgewater, formerly Fellow of Brasenose, was deprived for the same opinions. On leaving Oxford, Bridgewater retired to Douai, where, translating his name into "Aquapontanus," he became a Jesuit and gained considerable reputation as a theologian. About the same time, one, William Gifford, who had entered the College as a Commoner in 1570 and had been refused his degree as a "suspect," followed his Rector to the Continent, and afterwards, in 1622, became Archbishop of Reims and Primate of France. It was during Bridgewater's time in 1571, according to Brian Twyne, that the idea of ringing bells on "Coronation Day" originated. He says: "St. Hugh's day (Nov. 17) beinge a gaudy day in Lyncolne College, the masters and the other company after their gaudies and feastinge went to ringe at All hallowes, for exercise sake. Mr. Waite beinge then mayor of Oxford and dwellinge there-abouts, beinge much displeased with their ringinge (for he was a great precisian) came to the Church to knowe the cause of the ringinge. And at length beinge let in by the ringers, who had shut the doores privately to themselves, he demanded of them the cause of their ringinge, charginge them with popery, that they rang for a *dirige* for Queen Mary, etc., because she died upon that day. The most part answered that they did it for exercise ; but one seeinge his fellowes pressed by the mayor so neere, answered that they runge not for Queen Marie's *dirige* but for joy of Queen Elizabeth's coronation and that that was the cause of the ringinge. Whereuppon the mayor goinge away, in spite of that answer, caused Karfox bells to be runge, and the rest as many as he could command, and so the custom grewe." Another of these "gaudy" days which required so much exercise afterwards, was that of St. Mildred (July 13th), when they regaled themselves in 1550 "with wyne, cheares (i.e., cherries), and nutts" at a cost of 12d. These were not, however, the only occasions when the Fellows enjoyed themselves. They did a certain amount of entertaining of visitors who seem to have been tolerably frequent, sometimes in an official capacity and sometimes merely as friends. In 1576, there were great feastings with "venson pasties," "pigges," and "conyes," when Mr. Bodlye (perhaps the destined founder of the famous library) and Mr. Knolles (an ex-Fellow) came to dine. On each "count" day also (i.e., "the morrow of St. Thomas," or December 22nd, when the Bursar's books were audited) there were great potations which, in 1655 were supplemented by tobacco, then mentioned for the first time, while in 1669 they went so far as to start with "sider in the common chamber *the day before the accounts*"!

The chief result of the Reformation upon the College was the alteration of its former aims and objects, now illegal and prohibited, into that of the education of the young. This change was further brought about by the new regulations, which required that all undergraduates coming to the University should place themselves under a graduate tutor, and reside in one of the colleges or halls. From this time, therefore, dates the

INTRODUCTION

appearance of the "undergrad" proper in the life of the College. In 1552 there were in residence the Rector, eleven Fellows, one B.A. Commoner, and thirteen persons, not graduates, many of whom may have been private servitors, who would be getting their education in return for their services. By 1575 the Rector and Fellows had pupils assigned to them, who were presumably undergraduates, and in 1588 the College mustered the Rector, twelve Fellows, sixteen undergraduate Commoners, and nine servitors. From the small beginning the numbers rapidly increased, till we find that in 1605 the numbers were fifty-four, which in 1611 had jumped up to 101, and reached 109 the next year.

Among the men who about this time were elected to Fellowships must be noted Robert Sanderson, the famous logician and casuist, who entered the College in 1603, and took his degree three years later. He remained a Fellow for thirteen years, when he resigned to find preferment awaiting him. In 1631 he became Chaplain to Charles I, who used to say of him: "I carry my ears to other preachers, but I carry my conscience to hear Dr. Sanderson." In 1642 he was made Regius Professor of Divinity, and had the chief hand in drawing up the "Reasons" of the University for refusing to subscribe to the Solemn League and Covenant. At the Restoration he was made Bishop of Lincoln and reinstated in his Professorship, from which he had been ejected. He was possessed of a marvellous memory, but was so naturally nervous that he had to read all his sermons and speeches, and broke down in repeating the Lord's Prayer before one of his lectures.

Almost contemporary with him was Sir William Davenant, "the sweet swan of Isis," as Aubrey calls him, and Poet Laureate after Ben Jonson: he was born in Oxford, and in 1620 entered the College. He soon left, however, to go to Court, there to find a friend in Butler, of "Hudibras" fame, and a patron in Mr. Endymion Porter. He also fought on the side of Charles I, and was knighted for his services. After the

Restoration until his death in 1668 he spent his time writing plays, which were produced at his Playhouse in Lincoln's Inn Fields, now part of the Royal College of Surgeons.

During the first half of the seventeenth century the College buildings made good progress. The year 1607 saw the west side of the chapel quadrangle built, chiefly at the expense of Sir Thomas Rotheram, a former Fellow, and a member of the Founder's family. The account books show a total expenditure upon this new work of £251 16s. 8½d. The remainder of the quadrangle, consisting of the chapel and east side, was completed by the munificence of John Williams, Bishop of Lincoln, in the year 1629 and onwards, aided by contributions from, among others, Sir Peter Manwood, son of the founder of Sandwich School, of which something will be said later.

Although this period was thus notable for the increase both in numbers and accommodation, the record of the manners and morals of the time leaves much to be desired. The system of teaching by disputations, added to general intemperance, provoked heated discussions upon the absorbing political and religious topics of the day. These led to scenes of violence, and the annals show an unedifying picture of insolence to those in authority, of fighting between Fellows, and "desperate and barbarous assaults" of Commoners upon each other. A single example, taken from the College Register, will suffice: "Whereas there was a difference and falling out betwixt Mr. Kilbye and Mr. Webberlye (both Fellows) about yᵉ latter end of October laſt (1636), wherein there paſt ſome blowes on both ſydes . . . both of them were found corrigible by yᵉ Rector . . . and foraſmuch as no hurt or ſigne appeared upon Mr. Webberly, and it appeared that Mr. Kilbye his face was ſore bruiſed and beaten . . . and it could not appeare unto us but yᵗ Mr. Webberlye held Mr. Kilbye by yᵉ right hand when he ſtruck him firſt, to free himſelfe from him, it was further ordered that Mr. Webberly ſhould pay the charge of the Surgeon for healing of Mr. Kilbye's face."

INTRODUCTION

Archbishop Laud, who was Chancellor of the University from 1630 to 1641, endeavoured to put down the lawlessness that prevailed, but met with little success. He came into personal contact with the College by becoming its Visitor, on the suspension in 1639 of Bishop Williams. During his time of office, he had, on several occasions, to deal with cases of turbulence, and more especially in that of John Webberly before mentioned. This time, Webberly had been "sconced" by Paul Hood, the Rector, in the buttery book for riotous conduct, which sconce the former had "wiped off with irreverent and unbeseeming language." Webberly refused to sign the form of abject apology required by Hood, though he was ready to acknowledge his fault. Laud was willing to support Hood in his authority, but, at the same time, wrote to the Rector a wise letter, in which he said: "If you *will* hold him strictly to the form which you tendered him, I will do also. . . . Thus far I am very willing to go for the upholding of government. But my advice to you in private shall be this: that if he will give you a fair promise for the future, you should admit of the acknowledgment already made, and see how far that goodness will work upon him." A glance at Hood's thin, shifty-looking face in his portrait in the Hall, and it is not surprising to learn that he was too mean to meet his subordinate half-way.

It is a relief to turn from such sordid tales to the stirring events which so quickly followed. In 1642 the Civil War broke out, the University declared for the King, and for the next few years Oxford became an armed camp. There is no need to repeat at length the history of this time. At first, the city was held by the King, and the University and Colleges supplied both men and money with alacrity, though, no doubt, in the case of Puritan colleges, such as Lincoln had now become, the contribution was not as great as it might have been. This would appear to have been the case, judging from an entry in the accounts of "2 *subsidies* to the King" which amounted to 6s. 9d. ! After the Battle of Edgehill, in October, 1642, Charles made Oxford his head-quarters, and the colleges gave shelter to his officers and soldiery. Lincoln took its turn with the rest and housed Dr. Sibthorpe, the King's Chaplain, Sir Henry Radley, Sir Edward Wardor, and others, all of whom evidently paid something towards their keep, as the Bursar acknowledges small sums "from the strangers." Frequent calls for money had to be met. Contributions were made to Prince Rupert's trumpeters, "to his Maties drummers," and towards "the trenches about the towne." This duty of fortifying the city with earthworks was a task, which, owing to the lukewarmness of the town, fell chiefly on the colleges. It was a difficult business and lengthy, so much so, that in 1643 every resident in a college or hall, between the ages of sixteen and sixty, was ordered to work at them one day a week, or pay a shilling for a substitute. In 1645, the account books show "for 2 moneths' workinge at bulworks £1," and, of course, teem with other military references such as : " For keepinge a soldier, moneth (i.e., for one month) 17s. 6d.," "for a prayer at the beseiginge of Bristole," " D^{oo} Regi pro militibus £3," against which the Rector innocently added in the margin "to be paide againe," (1646) "pay^d to the Collectors for the souldiers £2 18s. 6d." During the absence of the regular army in the field, two regiments of volunteers were enrolled as a garrison. Lincoln supplied five men, including John Webberly, the refractory Fellow, but a staunch Royalist, and Thomas Marshall, afterwards Rector. The College also in 1645 and 1646 got in large quantities of "wheat and biefe (i.e., beef) for the siedge" which was then expected, but in the latter year the city surrendered to Fairfax. Some of the Fellows and Scholars took the opportunity of retiring abroad till things should become more settled, and among them Thomas Marshall, who went as Chaplain to the English merchants at Dordrecht.

Parliament now tried by a Commission of Visitors to overcome the resistance of the University. Lincoln at the time provided a strange medley of opinions, for the year that saw Robert Crosse, one of its Puritan Fellows, made Proctor, saw also the irrepressible John Webberly, then Sub-Rector, "affront and abuse" the Visitors, and expelled, with nine others, from his Fellowship. The majority of the Commoners of the College submitted to the Visitation, and the University Matriculation Register shows that in 1650 twenty-seven new undergraduates entered the College. It was, however, in the filling of the vacant Fellowships that the Commonwealth did harm to Lincoln. Not only did they expel by force those who would not submit, but they used the same means to foist upon the College men for the most part of evil character, the nominees of wire-pullers in London, who cared neither for the statutes nor the morals of the College, so that once again "rude, disturbing noises, unbecoming a college," resounded through the quadrangles. Other changes, too, were seen, as, for instance, in the chapel services, where, now that the old forms were abolished, extempore praying had been substituted, conducted by any member of the College, even undergraduates, who had a fancy to do so. Attempts were made at the same time to enforce a stricter mode of living, and 6s. 8d. was exacted for every indulgence in a curse.

There is an echo of the war to be found in the accounts for 1655, when they "paid to the beedle for maintenance of the raised troop 16s. 9d.," and bought "a sadle for the college troope-horse." This was in answer to the summons of Oliver Cromwell, then Chancellor of the University, for a garrison to hold Oxford for the Parliament when the Royalists were moving in the West of England. The promptness with which the militia turned out shows how completely the recent drastic measures had purged the city of the Cavalier element.

Brighter times dawned for Lincoln with the Restoration. In 1660 Charles "came to his own again," and the College paid 9s. 8d. "for fagots the coronation day." A Royal Commission was appointed to visit the University, expel the intruders, and, as far as possible, restore things as they were before. An interesting point then arose as to who should be made Vice-

Chancellor. The existing holder of the office had been ejected as being a Parliamentarian, and it was then found that all the other Heads of Houses, with the sole exception of Paul Hood, had been invalidly appointed during the recent troubles. Hood alone had been duly elected and admitted long before the rebellion began, and, therefore, it was absolutely necessary that, though old, infirm, and almost blind, he should fill the office, which no one else could do without their invalid headship being thereby confirmed. The Commission met with comparatively little resistance except in Lincoln, owing, perhaps, to the bad characters recently intruded into the College. They were, however, expelled after some little trouble, and their places filled by others of no particular note. Lord Clarendon, Chancellor in 1661, finally cleared the University of the opposing faction by his Act of Uniformity, and some Lincoln Fellows resigned their positions to avoid the otherwise inevitable expulsion.

An idea of the size of the College at this period may be obtained from a note in 1662 apropos of the imposition of the "chimney money" tax. This was 1s. charged half-yearly on every hearth in all houses above 20s. annual value. Lincoln returned fifty-two fireplaces, the smallest but two in the University.

The account books have two references to current events : "A treatment for the Visitors (i.e., the Commission) in the Hall, bisket, a quart of Canary and two of burnt claret," and "to Dr. Dolbin toward the intended entertainment of his Majesty £3 5s." This entertainment was duly given when Charles II, in 1663, paid his State visit to Oxford. The Senior Proctor that year was Nathaniel Crewe, Sub-Rector of Lincoln, and afterwards the greatest benefactor the College ever had. It was his duty to read the address of welcome to the King, who was so pleased that he wished to knight him on the spot, and promotion soon followed for one who was not only the son of a wealthy man, but had all the necessary accomplishments of a courtier. Crewe had always been a staunch Royalist, and, with his father, had been enthusiastic in working for the Restoration, and had showed his leanings to the old order of things by being the first to appear at chapel in a surplice. For the last few years of Hood's life Crewe had taken the lead in Lincoln, and when the aged Rector died in 1668, he was at once summoned from Court to accept the headship of the College. His Rectorship only lasted four years, but during that short time he made immense improvements in Lincoln. The general tone of the College became better, the numbers of under-graduates maintained a good average, the finances, by careful administration and many benefactions, were made stronger, and the buildings more comfortable with internal fittings. In 1672 Crewe resigned his office and returned to Court, but he never forgot Lincoln, with which his affection kept him in continual contact. For many years his advice was sought on momentous questions, and his influence was exerted for the good of his College, as, for example, in the election of Fellows. His father before him, John Crewe, Baron Stene, had fitted up the old chapel as the Library and turned the former Library into a fine set of rooms, and Nathaniel himself was even more generous. Towards special expenses he always gave liberally, as in con-tributing £100 towards the wainscoting of the Hall, until, in 1717, he finally crowned his gifts with a magnificent benefaction of £474 6s. 8d. per annum, intended to increase the incomes of the Rector, Fellows, Chaplains, Scholars, and Bible-clerk, in addition to founding twelve new exhibitions of £20 each. As a man of learning and refined taste, for he was no mean scholar and musician, he could appreciate and use his wealth to the full, and in his last days could make himself a benefactor to his College in the same princely fashion as he had been all his life.

The high standard set by Crewe was worthily kept up by his five immediate successors. Thomas Marshall, who was elected through Crewe's influence, had, in his earlier days, distinguished himself during the Civil War, so much so, that on taking his degree the usual fees were remitted to him in recognition of his services. He was well known also as a learned Teutonic scholar. In his time the account books give us an interesting glimpse of the way the officers went, and how much they spent, during one of the College Progresses through its manors for the purpose of holding Courts and seeing that all was going well with its property. On the occasion in question they had to go to Kent, and the details begin at London. They first spent a shilling in "boating it to and from Southwark, when we took places in the Canterbury coach," and seem to have returned and passed the rest of the day in London, for they subsequently spent two shillings in "coach-hire into Southwark that night." There they put up at one of the numerous coaching inns, and, next morning, the four of them, namely, the Rector, the Bursar, and two Fellows, Mr. Radcliffe, the famous physician, and Mr. Ellis, started off on their journey. It was a good distance, and, no doubt, the drive gave them an appetite, so that the next entry is "bread and beer on the rode," obtained at some convenient stopping-place.   Rochester was reached in time for dinner, to which, no doubt, they did full justice, though 5s. 6d. was their total expenditure. By the time they got near their journey's end the sun was going down, and the travellers perched on the top were beginning to get chilly, so we find them spending eightpence on "burnt brandy when we came to Canterbury." Here they evidently made their head-quarters. Mr. Radcliffe went off to Whitstable, probably in connexion with the lands providing the maintenance of four poor scholars at Lincoln under the Joan Traps benefaction. The others coached to Sandwich, there, no doubt, to interview the "Mayor and Jurats" of that place with regard to the School. This connexion of the College with Sandwich Grammar School dated from its foundation, in the latter part of the sixteenth century, by Roger Manwood, Chief Baron of the Exchequer, and executor to Joan Traps above mentioned. He provided that the Master of the School should be nominated by the College, and the post was generally filled by a Fellow, who was always presented by the Corporation to one of the town churches in their gift. When their patronage was taken from them by Act of Parliament, the headmastership alone did not carry with it sufficient income to make it worth the while of any graduate to accept it. It was only in 1907, however, that the late Sub-Rector, Dr. Williams, resigned his place among the governing body of the School, and it is to be hoped that this connexion between the two "seats of learning" will never be allowed to lapse. College property in Kent was not extensive, and the "Progress" does not seem to have gone much beyond this point, so, having paid "the Canterbury bills for diet, lodging, and for horses to Whitstable, £3 18s. 2d.," they took their seats on the return coach, and, after an uneventful journey, in due course arrived in London. The fare was twelve shillings per head each way, excluding tips to the coachman and postillion. In earlier days they seem to have spent quite a large part of their time on horseback going up to London on business, "to the syses at Habington," or attending my lord of Lincoln about College matters wherever he might happen to be. During all their journeys they looked well after the "inner man," and one naïve entry charges for "drincke by the way *and before we went.*"

Marshall died in 1685, and in his will proved himself a generous benefactor to the College. He gave to our Library his invaluable collection of tracts "most concerning the late troubles in England," some of which are not to be found in the Bodleian or British Museum, and the pick of his MSS. to Bodley. With the exception of a few small bequests, he gave his entire property to Lincoln "to purchase lands for the maintenance of some poor scholars." Unfortunately, rent-charges were bought instead of lands as he had wished, with the result that the advantage to the College was not as great as it might have been. One of the rent-charges, which, however, are still paid, is interesting as being a charge of £14 per annum on the produce of the chestnut trees in the Forest of Dean.

Before passing on, brief mention must be made of the two

noted Lincoln men of the time, George Hickes and John Radcliffe. The former, the Non-Juror and afterwards Dean of Worcester, was Fellow, 1664-81, and Sub-Rector in 1675. He was put forward as a candidate for the Rectorship on Marshall's death, but his reputation as a Scandinavian scholar and man of learning could not make up for his overbearing manners, and he was not elected. His portrait hangs in the Hall, presented by his successful opponent, Fitzherbert Adams. John Radcliffe, Fellow from 1670-5, was an instance of the curious fatality which has led the College more than once to quarrel with its benefactors, although, perhaps, in this case it was justified. Radcliffe, as a physician, wanted Lincoln to give up theology in favour of medicine, but it was felt that the Statutes could not be thus completely set aside, and his suggestion was refused. It is an ill wind that blows nobody any good, and although the College did not receive the further bounty which it would otherwise have done, nevertheless, the University can point to his library of scientific books, the "Camera," and the Observatory, University College to additional buildings, and the city to the Infirmary.

Under Fitzherbert Adams (1685-1719) the good government of the College continued. In the first year of his Rectorship there was the excitement of Monmouth's rebellion in the West. The University militia were called out in readiness, the Lincoln contingent forming part of the fifth company, but, as is well known, the venture came to nothing, and the would-be soldiers were disappointed of their fight. About this time the idea of a Livings' Fund was started in order to supply the College with the means of patronage for the Fellows. The Fellowships were sufficiently remunerative to tempt men to cling to them, and hitherto there had been nothing in the College gift to induce resignation. An effort towards this object was now made, and by means of subscriptions and gifts a sum was raised to buy, among others, the advowsons of Great Leighs, Essex; Winterborne, Dorset; Waddington, Lincs; and Cublington, Bucks.

INTRODUCTION

Lincoln has the satisfaction of knowing that she has supplied a Primate both to England and to France. The latter has already been mentioned in the account of William Gifford. To the former she gave John Potter, who had entered the College as a servitor in 1688. His rise was rapid. He was elected Fellow in 1694, Sub-Rector in 1703, and three years later took his D.D. degree. Two years afterwards he was made Regius Professor of Divinity; in 1715 Bishop of Oxford, in which capacity he ordained John Wesley; and in 1737 Archbishop of Canterbury.

With the death of Richard Hutchins (Rector, 1755-81), the period of good, if uneventful, government closes. Like Marshall, he left practically all he had to the College, because he said he owed it "entirely to the late Lord Crewe, by whose favour he obtained a Fellowship in Lincoln College, that he had anything now in his power to dispose of." He directed part of his property to be spent in buying the houses which lay between Lincoln and All Saints, thereby giving to the Fellows their present garden.

The history of the College for the fifty years following the death of Hutchins has very little of interest. Up to that time it had held a high position under a succession of capable Rectors, but afterwards the apathy and stagnation which were to be found throughout England were reflected also in the College life. Carelessness lost the College more than one benefaction, among others that of a rent-charge of £10 upon a house in the parish of St. Margaret's, Westminster, given by Sir George Wheler, to maintain a poor scholar from Wye Grammar School. Again, when the old College garden was taken, under the Act of 1771, to form part of the present city market, the compensation money was invested in the Funds, but the books were so badly kept that there were not sufficient details to enable the College to satisfy the authorities as to the justice of its claim to the investments, and Lincoln has the doubtful satisfaction of knowing that she has helped to build the Law Courts in the Strand.

INTRODUCTION

The last Rector of this period, Edward Tatham (1792-1834), was no better than his predecessors, and his claim to mention lies only in his marked peculiarities. He was of a coarse, blusterous character, which showed itself nowhere more clearly than in his bargain for a wife. Money was the essential point, and, discovering a retired builder at Gloucester, possessed of wealth and daughters none too beautiful, he addressed himself to the good man on the question of the dowry to be expected by a would-be son-in-law. Finding that the daughter least favoured by Nature would be the most favoured by her father, and having the amount of her "dot" quoted to him in pounds, Tatham brought his fist down on the table, saying, "Make it guineas, and I'm your man!" The bargain was struck, but in the end Tatham reaped where he had sown, and undergraduates used often to gather round outside their Rector's window to chuckle at the sounds of wordy warfare that issued forth. He came to loggerheads also with most of his contemporaries, and frequent lampoons were issued comparing him to the leaden imp which then "looked over Lincoln" from the niche in the tower on the quadrangle side. This was too much for Tatham, who had the figure taken down, whereupon a further lampoon told how that one night, when the Rector was returning from a dinner, "full of politics, learning, and port was his pate," the imp came down, made off with him, and came back to rule the College in his place. It is believed that the leaden figure was not destroyed, and, if that be so, is it too much to hope that possibly one day may see it restored to its original resting-place? It was during Tatham's Rectorship that Robert Montgomery, the poet, entered Lincoln as a Commoner. His vanity was colossal, and a fruitful source of practical jokes; in fact, he was even induced to go to the Vice-Chancellor and ask that his "viva" for "Smalls" might be postponed till the end of the vacation, "to avoid the inconveniences likely to be caused by the crowds which might be expected to attend his examination." He afterwards took an honorary fourth in "Greats."

INTRODUCTION

Tatham was succeeded in the Rectorship, after a contested election, by John Radford, who, though somewhat weak as a governor, took an intense pride in Lincoln, to which he was a considerable benefactor. It was most unfortunate that some of his bounty should have been applied in putting battlements upon the College buildings, thereby destroying their former picturesque appearance. His tomb, in All Saints, relates that "he dearly loved his College."

On his death, in 1851, there was again a keen contest for the headship. The issue lay at first between Mark Pattison and William Kay, but when the former's supporters saw that Kay was likely to be successful, they put forward James Thompson in his stead. He was gruff in manner and plain of speech, but, nevertheless, popular, and it was said of him that "He was always just. His acts of kindness being unexpected were the more valued." The chief point in his favour, and which, no doubt, helped his election, was that he was well acquainted with the estates and business of the College, a qualification not to be overlooked on the eve of a University Commission. His old opponent, Mark Pattison, succeeded him in 1861, and for twenty years the College rejoiced in having for Rector one of the most brilliant scholars of the day, who was "not only a storehouse of knowledge, but a matchless critic." He had been elected Fellow in 1839, and ordained Priest four years later. He was very regular in his attendance at Chapel, when he used to read slowly and with a drawl, while on surplice days he wore black gloves, being very sensitive to cold. Perhaps, as might be expected, he was not quite so successful a Rector as a less clever man might have been. He wished that the College might return somewhat to its old lines, and that the undergraduate might be banished in favour of the graduate student, whose life should be given up to research. Although this could be but an ideal, still such a feeling tended to cramp the work of the College, added to which he was a man of moods and a sharp tongue, at one time genial, at another sarcastic.

INTRODUCTION

In 1884 the thirtieth and present Rector, the Rev. William Walter Merry, D.D., was elected "unanimi consensu omnium suffragantium." He was a Scholar of Balliol, and Fellow of Lincoln since 1859. His name will be familiar enough to those who have read Homer and Aristophanes, and those who have heard him deliver the "Creweian Oration" at Commemoration will understand why he fills the post of Public Orator to the University. Dr. Merry was Vice-Chancellor in 1904-6, being the ninth supplied by the College to that office. His portrait, which forms the frontispiece to this book, was painted by Mr. Cyrus Johnson, and was exhibited in 1898 at the Royal Academy.

A full list of Rectors, with as many specimens of their respective signatures as could be found, is given at the end.

Lincoln has now reached that stage when expansion would make a vast difference to the College. The reason why Fleming chose St. Mildred's as being specially suited to make way for his College is to-day the very reason why Lincoln is hampered in her progress. Planted in a confined space and crowded in on all sides, she has no means of giving increased accommodation for students. It is true that within the last quarter of a century the buildings have been extended and alterations carried out which make a larger number of rooms available, but the result is not sufficient, and there is little or no space left on which to build. Though not one of the largest Colleges, Lincoln holds to-day as good a position in the University as ever it did, and it remains to be seen whether a way cannot be devised to overcome the present difficulty and make of it a College such as its Founder never dreamt, but as all its sons would have it be. For, whatever Fortune may have in store for Lincoln, to those who have spent their all too brief years at Oxford within its walls there will be no spot in the "City of Spires," however famous or however beautiful, which will recall itself so pleasantly to their memory as their ancient College in Turl Street.

LOOKING TOWARDS TRINITY

THE oriel window overlooking the Fellows' Garden marks the Chaplain's Room, and is associated in modern times with the name of Washbourne West, the wealthy Bursar, who died in 1897. It was said of him that when at Combe, near Woodstock, he had preached to the country yokels about "swearing at their ploughs," and that in later years he used this same sermon at All Saints, on the occasion of a heavy "plough" in "Smalls"! He was a strong Conservative, with no less than twenty-three votes, of which, in 1892, when aged eighty, he polled as many as seventeen. He was well known also for his whist parties, with five shilling points. Readers of the "Verney Memoirs" may remember the incident of the Westminster boy, Robert Uvedale, at Oliver Cromwell's funeral. On that occasion the "Majesty Scutcheon," a kind of pall placed on the coffin of Royalty, was also used for that of Cromwell. This so offended the boy's Royalist feelings that he dashed between the guards, snatched it from the bier, and escaped before he could be prevented. The relic was afterwards handed down in his family until it came to Washbourne West, whose mother was a direct descendant, and at his death it was, of course, dispersed with his estate elsewhere.

This is a specimen of the heads of the rain-water pipes of late eighteenth century design, with which the College is furnished throughout.

HEAD OF
RAIN - WATER
PIPE

LOOKING TOWARDS TRINITY COLLEGE

FRONT QUADRANGLE

THIS view shows the Front Quadrangle looking back upon the tower from the Rector's lodgings, with the plane tree in the College stable-yard peeping over the roof. It is the earliest part of Lincoln, with the probable exception of the kitchen, though somewhat spoilt by modern additions. The tower, where the Rectors originally lived, now contains a bed-room, with the muniment room above it, reached by a winding staircase and entered through a small door with three ponderous locks. Inside are the title-deeds to the College properties, together with other valuable documents, to not a few of which are attached the large round seals of various Sovereigns. Among other things are two fine specimens of iron-bound wooden chests, one of which is here reproduced. To the right, in the corner of the quadrangle, is the Fellows' Morning Room, formerly known as the "poste chamber," from a pedestal at the foot of the staircase, on which was a statue of St. Hugh of Lincoln. Above it is the Sub-Rector's Room, formerly the old library. In Loggan's view of the College it will be noticed that the windows were of two lights each, but Georgian taste wrought havoc with them.

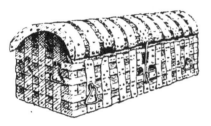

IRON-BOUND CHEST IN TOWER (16th cent.)

THE FRONT QUADRANGLE LOOKING TOWARDS THE ENTRANCE

FRONT QUADRANGLE

THE bell turret is modern. On the woodwork inside is carved, "Revd John Calcott Bursar MDCCCXXXVI," while the bell, which rings to Chapel and Hall, has this pertinent inscription round the edge, "Come away without delay. 1748." The staircase on the left leads up to what was the original Chapel. When the present one was built the old room remained disused until about 1655, when it was fitted up as the Senior Library. In 1906 its purpose was again altered, and it is now two stories, with ordinary rooms. The room on the ground floor is the Senior Common Room. Notice up in the wall the College "overseer," the Lincoln Imp, adopted from the figure in the Angel Choir in Lincoln Cathedral.

ORIGINAL LOUVRE OR SMOKE-HOLE (1437)

On the extreme right the very fine and original louvre, or smoke-hole, on the Hall should be remarked. This is a now uncommon relic of the days when the fire was in the middle of the room and the smoke was left to find its way out through the roof. When the ceiling of the Hall was uncovered in 1891 the woodwork of the hole was found to be begrimed with smoke, thus showing that it had duly fulfilled its purpose.

THE FRONT QUADRANGLE LOOKING TOWARDS THE HALL

RICHARD FLEMING

RICHARD FLEMING, our first Founder, was a native of Yorkshire and an Oxford man, having graduated from University College, and been Junior Proctor in 1407. In his early days he had been an ardent follower of Wyclif, but as he grew older his opinions changed. Anthony Wood thinks that they did so not so much from conviction as from worldly considerations, and certainly he was not left long without preferment. He first became Rector of Boston, Lincs, and was chosen to go as Ambassador to the Council of Sens, where he made a great impression. In 1415 he was made a Prebendary of York Cathedral, and four years later was promoted to the See of Lincoln, being consecrated at Florence the next year. Fleming was a favourite of Pope Martin V, who made him his Chamberlain, and in 1424 nominated him to be Archbishop of York. Henry VI, however, had already given his sanction to the election of the Bishop of Worcester, and Fleming was compelled to return ignominiously to Lincoln. His portrait shows him full face, crosier in hand, but it is by no means certain that the features are authentic.

His case goes to prove that the pre-Reformation Bishops were not as wealthy as is generally supposed, for it is noticeable that Fleming only gave churches as endowment for his new foundation, and contributed little or nothing from his private means.

RICHARD FLEMING, BISHOP OF LINCOLN

SENIOR COMMON ROOM

UNTIL the year 1662 the Fellows had nowhere to go in the evenings for a quiet talk or friendly gathering, except to some neighbouring tavern or the Hall among the undergraduates, where the "common fire," the only fire in College, was lighted in the middle of the room at five o'clock on winter nights. In this year the present room, below the old Chapel, as already mentioned, was set apart "for the use of the Fellows for their common fyres." In 1684 it was handsomely wainscoted, at a cost of about £95. The chairs date from 1815. Here is preserved the old College warming-pan, of the usual kind and rather battered, in which the ashes of the fire were placed when the Fellows retired to rest, and which was then taken round by the porter to warm their beds in order of seniority.

UPPER STAIRCASE

This is the upper portion of the staircase leading up by the Sub-Rector's Room, and dates from about the year 1656. On the way up may be also noticed one of the old small fifteenth century windows, with cusped head, now partly walled up.

THE SENIOR COMMON ROOM

THE FELLOWS

AS constituted by Rotheram the College was to consist of a Rector and twelve Fellows, but the number varied greatly, and, until about 1630, was generally less. Before the substitution of open Fellowships by the University Commission of 1854, they had been confined to natives of certain parts of the country, viz., four to Lincolnshire, four to Lincoln Diocese (the three "Darby" Fellows were taken out of these later on), two to Yorkshire, two to York Diocese, and one to Wells Diocese (this last in memory of our benefactor, John Forrest, Dean of Wells). The thirteenth Fellowship (one of the two assigned to York Diocese) was permanently annexed to the Rectorship. Originally their chief duties were to assist the Chaplains, collect alms and fees for the Bursar, and attend the University courses of work. They were also obliged to proceed, in due course, to their B.D. degree. Their income at this time was very poor. They only had their "commons," or weekly allowance of food, their rooms rent free, "obits," or small money allowances for presence at Mass on keeping the anniversary of some benefactor's death; "pittances," or small sums, also derived from bequests by benefactors; and a "salary," which was also a small money payment. As, however, each source only yielded a few shillings, the sum total did not amount to very much. When undergraduates were admitted matters improved. About the close of the sixteenth century stipends were paid, in addition, to certain Fellows for giving special tuition, i.e., the lecturers in theology, Greek, philosophy (who supervised the work of B.A.'s reading for M.A.), and logic (who attended to the disputations of undergraduates for B.A.). In those days the tutors had each a number of undergraduates assigned to them, and were responsible for their education and conduct. Furthermore, they managed their financial affairs, paying their battels and tradesmen's bills with money which had to be deposited at the beginning of term. The tutors were thus said to give "caution" for their pupils. That this system was strongly disliked is not surprising, and in the Roxborough Ballads may be found these rhymes, which probably voiced the general feeling on the subject.

* * * * * *

"And then a Tutor we must have.

"This Fellow sends unto our friends
To keepe our money for his own ends;
And there he locks it in his truncke
Whilst we must upon ticke be druncke.

"We never ask him for a groate,
But wish 'twere all stucke in his throate,
Till at length, at Quarter's Day, there comes
The dunners with their bouncing summes."

This system, too, may have especially rankled when even the tutors themselves seem to have deserved a little supervision, for in 1550 there was charged 18d. for "Sir Atkyns' (a Fellow) commons when he was in bocardo" (i.e., the debtors' prison over the north gate)!

In modern days, of course for teaching purposes only, undergraduates are still assigned to tutors, according to the branch of study upon which they intend to enter, while in place of the "Quarter's Day" and the "dunner" there is the reckoning to be paid, by the undergraduate, at "Collections," when the tutor makes his report on the term's work. These same "Collections" were first instituted in 1828, "for the improvement of College discipline, as well as to ascertain the progress of the Undergraduates in literature."

THIS fine interior is the Dining Room in the Rector's lodgings, and shows the original panelling and cross-beams. Particular attention should be paid to the magnificently-carved mantelpiece. From its general style and complete undercutting, it would seem to have been done by the same hand as the carving in the Chapel, and the fact that the execution is so good makes it a matter for regret that the carver is unknown. Another well-wrought mantelpiece is in the

MANTELPIECE IN THE RECTOR'S DINING ROOM

Drawing Room upstairs, but is not to be compared with its rival below. Underneath is a large cellar, where they used to store fish for Lent, and in which the Rector, Dr. Cottisford, as Vice-Chancellor, in 1527, imprisoned some Lutheran suspects, with the result that many eventually died from the bad air.

The Rector's lodgings were originally only the continuation of the Hall, and it was not until 1630 that the staircase on the chapel quadrangle was annexed in consequence of the Rector being married.

THE RECTOR'S DINING ROOM

THE COLLEGE ARMS

LINCOLN has an interesting coat of arms, which were ratified, confirmed, and recorded, if not made, in the year 1574, by Richard Lee, Portcullis Pursuivant, at his visitation of the University.* The coat has three quarterings. The first is naturally Fleming's arms : (1) " Barry of six argent and azure, in chief three lozenges gules, on the fess point a mullet sable." The second shows those of the See of Lincoln, denoting that our Founders were its Bishops : (2) "Gules, two lions passant gardant or, on a chief azure Our Lady sitting wit her Babe, crowned and sceptred or, the whole ensigned with mitre." The third bears, as it should do, the arms of Rotherar our second Founder : (3) "Vert three stags trippant or (? arg.)

It is a moot point whether Lee found these arms already existence or whether he invented them himself, though it generally considered that the latter is the more probable. F. original parchment certificate with the arms upon it blazoned colour and stained with age, is stuck inside the cover of . second volume of the College Register. Owing to their intric mistakes are frequently made in reproducing the arms, the n' common being to depict a demi-lady instead of the Virgin sea

In spite of Lee's blazon the colour of the stags' Rotheram's coat of arms has been questioned. In four sepa: Heraldic Visitations they are given as "or," but it has rece. been found that on the first page of the Statutes of his Col' of Jesus in Yorkshire, probably written soon after his de and now preserved in the library of Sidney Sussex Coll Cambridge, they appear to be represented as "arg." with.' motto "Da te Deo." This, however, does not seem to be 4' certain, and it has been thought best to reproduce the : exactly as given to the College by Lee.

The Mitre has been taken as the College crest, and the College colours are dark and light blue.

* The account books show that the College gave in this year "to the harold of armes at his visitation in Oxford, 20s."

THE COLLEGE ARMS

THE COLLEGE ARMS

LINCOLN has an interesting coat of arms, which were ratified, confirmed, and recorded, if not made, in the year 1574, by Richard Lee, Portcullis Pursuivant, at his visitation of the University.* The coat has three quarterings. The first is naturally Fleming's arms : (1) " Barry of six argent and azure, in chief three lozenges gules, on the fess point a mullet sable." The second shows those of the See of Lincoln, denoting

THE COLLEGE ARMS—AN AMENDMENT

IT is only too true that ' mistakes are frequently made ' with regard to the arms, and unfortunately the author has been no exception !

In the first place the trick in colour shown here of the ' arms as given by Lee ' is inaccurate in these respects, viz. :—The field of the centre pale should be ' argent' not ' azure,' for the latter involves the heraldic fault of colour on colour, and, further, the stags should be shown as ' statant,' not ' trippant.'

In the second place, although it cannot be distinguished in Lee's trick, there is not much doubt but that, as the College seal shows, the mullet should be pierced. This at least as far as the College arms are concerned, although it is open to argument (which can be supported by MS. evidence) that the mullet in Fleming's private coat apart from the College may not have been so pierced.

From an authoritative trick in colour recently (1920) obtained from the College of Arms, and from what can be made out with difficulty from Lee's parchment, the arms should be blazoned as follows :—(1) ' Barry of six argent and azure in chief three lozenges gules on the fess point a mullet sable pierced ' (Fleming) ; (2) ' On a field argent the arms of the See of Lincoln as described opposite ' ; (3) ' Vert three stags statant or ' (Rotheram). Beyond these two authorities it is not necessary to go as regards the arms for the College, but as a point of academic interest it may be noted that really weighty authorities can be produced to support the various combinations of stags trippant argent, trippant or and trippant argent attired or. These suggest that, while we must accept Lee's blazon for the College, he may have been himself in error (as well he might be !) in respect of the tincture and posture of the stags in Rotheram's private coat.

Since the publication of this book the author has consulted many printed works, an even larger number of MSS. at the Bodleian and British Museum libraries, Queen's College, Oxford, and Caius and Sidney Sussex Colleges, Cambridge, and various other sources of information, without any other result than to add to the numbers of authorities for each respective combination above mentioned !

notto "Da te Deo." This, however, does not seem to be quite certain, and it has been thought best to reproduce the arms exactly as given to the College by Lee.

The Mitre has been taken as the College crest, and the College colours are dark and light blue.

* The account books show that the College gave in this year "to the harold of armes at his visitation in Oxford, 20s."

THE COLLEGE ARMS

THE COLLEGE SEALS

THE small oval seal fixed to a handle shows the figure of St. Hugh of Lincoln with "🏵 **hugo**" beneath, and round the edge "**Sigillum Collegii Lyncolne in Oronia ad causas.**" This is used for stamping letters-testimonial and documents of minor importance.

The chief or "common" seal, intended for use with a press, has been submitted to the authorities at the British Museum, to whom it was unknown, for their opinion. The Virgin is seated in the middle, with the Holy Trinity above. (Extract from opinion) "The inscription appears to read: '**S**(igillum) **Co**(mmun)**e rectoris et Collegat**(um) **Collegii Beatae Mariae et om**(n)**i**(um) **s**(an)**c**(t)**o**(rum) **Lincolnie i**(n) **Oronia.**' The persons represented under the canopies on the two sides are—on the right, or sinister, side: (1) Moses and St. John the Baptist. (2) St. Stephen and St. Lawrence. (3) St. Katharine and St. Margaret. On the left, or dexter, side

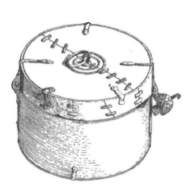

IVORY BOX FOR COMMON SEAL

are: (1) Two angels in Amices and girded Albs. (2) St. Peter and St. Paul. (3) Two Bishops, one of whom should be St. Hugh of Lincoln, the other perhaps St. Richard, since the founder of the College was Bishop Richard Fleming, whose arms are in base." The large seal is kept in this ivory box. Both the seals are silver, and date from the fifteenth century.

THE COLLEGE SEALS

(ACTUAL SIZE)

THOMAS ROTHERAM AND
COLLEGE STATUTES

OUR second Founder, born in 1423, was a man of considerable reputation. He may possibly have been an Eton
boy, but is first definitely heard of at King's College,
Cambridge. He subsequently become Provost of Beverley and
Bishop of Rochester. In 1467 he was made Keeper of the
Privy Seal, and the following year Ambassador to the King of
France. He became Chancellor of Cambridge University in
1469, and three years later was translated to the See of Lincoln,
when his connexion with Oxford first
begins. He was also Lord High Chancellor
of England and afterwards Archbishop of
York. In his portrait it will be noticed
that Rotheram has been given the triple
or papal cross by mistake, while the doubt
as to its authenticity applies to this picture
equally as to that of Fleming. Tradition
has it that Bishop Sanderson gave these
two portraits to the College.

STONE ANGEL BEARING
ROTHERAM'S ARMS

It has been already told how nobly Rotheram fulfilled his
promise of help. Not only did he rescue Lincoln from destruction, but he increased the number of Fellowships by five, and
enlarged its funds by incorporating the rectories of Long

42

THOMAS ROTHERAM, ARCHBISHOP OF YORK

Combe in Oxfordshire and Twyford in Bucks. Furthermore, in 1480 he gave the statutes, still preserved in an unpretentious-looking parchment booklet tied with green silk and approved by his signature. Under these statutes, which were substantially the governing force of the College till 1854, the Rector was to be a highly privileged person, acting as Rector of the mother churches, now four in number, and in receipt of considerable emoluments. The Fellows were to be thirteen in number, as before mentioned, and the Chaplains four, to serve the churches, each receiving a stipend of £5 per annum. The Chaplaincies and the College servants will be more fully mentioned later. There was also to be a Bible-clerk, originally chosen from the choristers of Lincoln Cathedral, who was to act as the Rector's servant, and say grace and read passages from the Bible or other instructive book during meals. Rotheram also refers to Commoners or " sojourners." These were probably M.A.'s not on the foundation, who merely came to the College for purposes of study, and arrangements are made for their attendance at the University disputations and for their discipline generally. In 1637 there were eight of them in residence, but very little seems to be known about them.

THE FOUNDERS' TOMBS

OPPOSITE are the Founders' tombs. The upper that of Fleming in Lincoln Cathedral, the lower that of Rotheram in York Minster. The latter was destroyed in Martin's fire of 1829, and carefully copied and restored in 1830 by the College under the superintendence of Mr. Skelton, F.S.A. It is interesting to note that in 1735 a wooden head, which may possibly have been carried in his funeral procession, on the analogy of the wax figures in Westminster Abbey, was found in Rotheram's tomb, and is now preserved in the Minster.

FLEMING'S TOMB, LINCOLN CATHEDRAL

ROTHERAM'S TOMB, YORK CATHEDRAL

THE CHAPEL QUADRANGLE

BEARING to the right on entering the College, a narrow passage leads into the chapel quadrangle. Originally this part was occupied by Hampton and Sekyll Halls, bought from University College in 1463. The side facing on to the Turl was built in 1607, and the Chapel and rooms on the east side about twenty-three years later. These two sides are the only part of the College to escape the disfiguring battlements, and show how charming Lincoln must have looked in its original style. The vine is seen flourishing on the walls, and on the left the window over the archway marks the room which John Wesley is traditionally reported to have used when Fellow. In the corner are the Rector's lodgings, and next door is No. 8 staircase, which has had some well-known inhabitants in its time, among others Mark Pattison (who had meetings there with J. H. Newman, Dean Church, and Charles Marriott), James Fraser (Bishop of Manchester), Bishop Jacobson, and the Right Honourable Viscount Morley, of Blackburn, present Secretary of State for India. "No. 6 ground floor right" was the room assigned to the Bible-clerk.

Below are specimens of tiny grotesques under the archway leading into the Turl.

GROTESQUES IN CHAPEL QUADRANGLE GATEWAY

46

THE CHAPEL QUADRANGLE

JOHN WESLEY

ONE of the chief attractions of the College to visitors is its connexion with John Wesley. This brilliant man, born in 1703, was educated at Charterhouse, and early showed great promise, being spoken of, at the age of sixteen, "as a scholar and learning Hebrew." He came up to Christ Church in 1720, took his degree in 1724, was ordained the next year in the Cathedral, and preached his first sermon at South Leigh, near Witney. In 1726 he obtained a Lincoln Fellowship. His time at first was taken up with his work as tutor and also as curate for his father in his Lincolnshire parish, while he afterwards joined his brother and others at Christ Church in their religious society. On his marriage in 1751 he gave up his Fellowship, and his resignation is reproduced from the College Register. His portrait hangs in the Hall, and shows him in his younger days, with slim figure and fresh complexion. It has been examined by Sir Charles Robinson and pronounced authentic and genuine, but the painter is unknown.

JOHN WESLEY'S RESIGNATION OF HIS FELLOWSHIP

THE REV. JOHN WESLEY, M.A.

THE CHAPEL

THE present Chapel was consecrated in 1631 by the Bishop of Oxford, acting under commission from Bishop Williams, and is generally considered to be a very good

JOHN WESLEY'S PULPIT

specimen of | what is known
as " Jacobean | Gothic." On
entering the | Chapel the first
thing that | strikes the
visitor is the | peculiarly
fragrant smell, | due to the fact
that all the | woodwork is
made of cedar. | This internal
decoration | was added in
1686 by the | generosity of
Fitzherbert | Adams, and
shows some | very fine carv-
ing. In the | ante-chapel
stands the pul- | pit from which
John Wesley | used to preach,
and a small | brass on the
panelling at | the west end
keeps alive the | memory of
Edward Grin- | field, the

founder of the Septuagint Lectureship in the University.

Passing through the beautifully carved screen, the chief thing that arrests the attention is the fine glass filling the

THE CHAPEL SCREEN

THE CHAPEL

windows, which will be fully explained later on. The walls are panelled all round for

a height of about eight feet, and above the altar is a carved and gilded garland, composed of roses, wheat-ears, lilies, and vine-clusters. On the ends of the stalls are set well-executed figures of Moses and Aaron at the east end, the four Evangelists in the middle, and St. Peter and St. Paul at the west end. The gift of the Chapel is recited at the end of the College Bidding Prayer, in which the names of our greatest benefactors are kept in remembrance. For the purpose of reading the lessons in Chapel on Sunday evenings two undergraduates are annually chosen for the office, to which

a small money prize is attached which has to be expended on books. For the daily lessons Lincoln is unusual in that all the undergraduates are obliged to read in turn, whereas in the majority of other colleges this duty is confined to scholars.

It has been mentioned that it had been the custom to use the Chapel for declamations and other secular exercises, and during the Commonwealth for any person to conduct the services who liked to do so, and this seems to have continued until 1699,

ST. LUKE

when the College register shows an order that "From henceforward no Fellow nor any other person shall presume to read prayer in the Chapel, except he be in Priest's or Deacon's orders." In 1796 a Chaplain was appointed "to do the ordinary duty of the Chapel" at a stipend of £40 per annum.

The College had four Chaplains attached who served the collegiate churches of All Saints', St. Michael's, Twyford, and Combe Longa. These chaplaincies were, in a sense, Peculiars, for they were not

ST. JOHN

ST. PAUL

under the jurisdiction of the Ordinary, but under that of the Rector, who had complete control over them, and not only so, but they were neither instituted by the Bishop

ST. PETER

nor inducted by the Archdeacon. In 1833 the College came into opposition with and actively resisted Samuel Wilberforce, Bishop of Oxford, who tried to assert his jurisdiction over them. However, the Ecclesiastical Jurisdiction Act of 1847 abolished the system of Peculiars, and from that date the exclusive connexion of the College with its Churches came to an end.

It is interesting to note that for a long time it was the fashion for the parishioners of Combe Longa to celebrate their weddings in the College Chapel, which were, however, recorded in the register of their own Church. The floors also of both the Chapel and ante-chapel were consecrated for burial purposes, though they do not appear ever to have been so used, as the tombs in All Saints' and St. Michael's testify; and whether any baptisms were celebrated here or not is also uncertain, all traces of the font having long since vanished.

WOOD CARVING OVER THE ALTAR

THE CHAPEL INTERIOR

THE CHAPEL GLASS

FOR extraordinary detail and immense perspective this east window will be difficult to excel, and will well repay close inspection. It is divided into two parts, of six lights each, setting forth Types below and Antitypes, or scenes from Our Lord's life, above. Starting on the left, the lights show: (i) The Creation and the history of Adam and Eve; (I) the Birth of Our Lord. (ii) The children of Israel pursued by the Egyptians (the pillars of ruby-red cloud are considered very good pieces of glass); (II) the Baptism of Our Lord. (iii) The Passover; (III) the Last Supper (Our Lord sits at the head with, curiously enough, the Virgin Mary at His right hand). (iv) The Brazen Serpent; (IV) the Crucifixion. (v) The story of Jonah; (V) the Resurrection. (vi) Elijah caught up to Heaven (notice especially the immense distance portrayed in this light); (VI) the Ascension. The tracery of the window is filled with various architectural designs. The side windows are rather different in design, and contain large single figures of Old Testament Prophets on the north and the twelve Apostles on the south side. The latter form what is known as a "Creed" window, each Apostle being said to have contributed a clause to the Creed, and having it here written beneath him. The tracery of these contains the arms of Bishop Williams, the Deanery of Westminster, and the See of Lincoln. The canopies and character of the writing have been thought especially fine. The glass is of the painted kind, and the prevailing colours in the east window are yellow, green, and blue, those in the side windows being more varied and richer in depth of colouring, with the result that the general effect is more harmonious and less crude in tone than in some of the examples mentioned below. The east window is dated 1631, and those on the south side 1629 and 1630, but the north lights do not appear to have any date.

THE CHAPEL : EAST WINDOW

THE CHAPEL GLASS

This is a specimen of one of the windows on the north side, and shows Malachi on the left, Zacharias in the centre, and Amos on the right. The canopies, though rather exuberant in design, together with the large flowing robes of the figures, have given the artist a good opportunity of displaying his colouring to the best advantage. Each prophet holds some object emblematic of his career: thus Amos has his shepherd's crook; and of the others who are not shown may be mentioned Obadiah, with three large flat pieces of bread and a gorgeous ewer; Ezekiel holding a model of the Temple; Elijah with a sword, and a priest of Baal at his feet; and David with his harp and ermine robe. In the background is the interior of an ecclesiastical building, and beneath each figure is an explanatory Latin couplet. In 1663 the glass had to be repaired, as may be seen in one or two places; and in 1772 Peter Davis, whose name occurs among the plate, gave money for wiring over the glass, which involved an expense of £106 9s., the surplus from his gift being kept to purchase ground for augmenting the College.

It is unfortunate that the authors of the two most interesting features in the Chapel, the carving and the glass, are unknown. Tradition, based on Anthony Wood, has it that Williams brought this glass from Italy, but there is no actual evidence to support the theory. On the other hand, a careful comparison with the glass at Queen's, Wadham, and University Colleges leads strongly to the conclusion that they are all the work of the same hand. That in the Colleges mentioned is definitely known to have been made by the brothers Van Linge, who especially flourished in Oxford during this period. English authorities also, such as Messrs. Westlake, Winston, and others, incline to the belief that it is the work of these men, and in each case mention the glass in Archbishop Abbot's Hospital at Guildford, which is dated 1621, and bears an even stronger resemblance to the Lincoln windows than the others quoted, though unfortunately its author is also unknown. It has been said that the artist was a relation of the Archbishop.

THE CHAPEL : NORTH WINDOW

THE CHAPEL FROM THE GARDEN

THIS view of the Chapel is taken from the Fellows' Garden, a small plot lying between the College and All Saints', formerly covered by houses, with a narrow lane running down by the churchyard. The oriel window on the left is modern work, but harmonizes well with the building to which it is attached. The roof of the Chapel was formerly covered with Stonesfield slates, the product of an Oxfordshire quarry, and similar to those in the quadrangle adjoining, but their weight was found to be too great for the timbers, and the ordinary slate had to be substituted.

THE BÂTON

The " Bamboo," or bâton, is a stout piece of bamboo about 6 ft. 9 in. high and 1¼ in. in diameter, with a once gilded iron top. When the present Chapel was built, Bishop Williams dispensed with the attendance of the College at the services in All Saints' Church as hitherto prescribed by the Statutes. It was, however, arranged that on All Saints' Day the Rector and Fellows should go in procession to the Church, when the porter used to walk in front, carrying the " Bamboo." After the separate jurisdiction of the College over the Church had come to an end the procession, by permission of the Visitor, in 1866 was finally discontinued.

THE
COLLEGE
BÂTON

THE CHAPEL FROM THE FELLOWS' GARDEN

THE LIBRARY

FOR the third time the Library moved into a new abode when, in 1906, this handsome building was erected at the end of the Fellows' Garden from the design of Messrs. Read and Mackenzie. The College owes it largely to the generous legacy left by the late Dr. Thomas Fowler, President of C.C.C., and for many years Fellow, Tutor, and Sub-Rector of Lincoln, for which reason the Pelican has been included in the details of the decoration, together with the Imp and the Mitre. The upper floor is the Senior Library, fitted with the oak shelves from the old room, which were bought in 1739 with the £500 given by Sir Nathaniel Lloyd, which purchase for some reason or other so roused his ire that he refused to give anything more to the College. The ground floor is the Junior Library, and comprises all the books which were formerly kept in the old Junior Library on No. 9 staircase (now the Junior Common Room), and in the old Wesley Lecture Room (now an undergraduate room), the former of which contained the classical authors and the latter chiefly works on modern history. Adjoining the main portion of the building on the left is a Lecture Room, which, together with the Library itself, is reached by a long passage from the Grove.

Donations of books have been frequent and varied, beginning with the MSS. given by Fleming and William Chamberleyn, the first Rector. One of those presented by Fleming is of the twelfth century, and formerly belonged to the Priory of St. Cuthbert of Worksop, and there is also another in Greek, probably of the eleventh century, which was once the property of the "priest of St. Michael's." He also gave one very significant volume, when the change in his religious opinions is remembered, namely, "Walden contra Wyclyff," which is mentioned in 1521 as having been wrapped in "an ell off canvass" and sent up to London, perhaps to do battle once again for the old faith at that troublous time. In 1432

THE LIBRARY

THE LIBRARY

Dr. Thomas Gascoigne gave six MSS., and in the seventeenth century the College acquired his "Liber Veritatum," or Theological Dictionary, a well-written MS. with coloured initial letters, containing scraps of ecclesiastical and other information,

and among other things a mention of Chaucer. Further gifts included that of thirty-eight MSS. in 1465 from Robert Fleming, Dean of Lincoln, a relation of the Founder and a great traveller in Italy and elsewhere. For the restoration under Rotheram a valuation of the College had to be made, and although that has unfortunately been lost, there is still preserved the inventory of books chained in the Library in 1474 showing that there were then 134 MSS., thirty-seven of which were lent out to Fellows. These, of course, are not all in the possession of the College to-day. Mention of chains in the accounts is frequent, for instance in 1550, "for cheynynge the books 18d."; but such things were of no avail against the depredations, for example, of Edward VI's Commissioners in their zeal for the destruction of "superstitious books," and although it is not definitely known how much actual damage was done to Lincoln Library, in common with the rest, there can be little doubt but that the strong words of Anthony Wood, apropos of the Libraries, "suffering thereby such an incredible damage that posterity have cursed their proceedings," were fully justified in our particular case. Neither did the chains prevent Commoners in the seventeenth century, who had gained access to the Library, from mutilating the books by cutting out the illuminated initial letters and borders, as Gascoigne's MS. itself bears witness, and putting them in their scrap albums. All MSS. have now, however, been deposited in the Bodleian for the purposes of safe custody and of affording an easier means of reference for readers.

Printed books have been given in large numbers by benefactors from Edmund Audley to modern times. Of these, the most important are Marshall's tracts and pamphlets of the Stuart period and a collection of eighteenth century plays. Several other volumes are worthy of remark, one being the translation of the Bible attributed to Wyclif, with red and blue illumination; another Bible, given by Nathaniel Crewe,

SMALL STRONG-BOX IN LIBRARY (16th cent.)

bearing on the cover in several places the royal crown and Charles II's monogram of two interlacing C's; and yet a third of the seventeenth century, interleaved and containing references and comments, written in a neat, but microscopic, hand in Greek, Latin, Hebrew, and English. It also has an ingenious kind of index, formed of hundreds of tiny tags of parchment, stuck on to, and projecting from, the leaves. In 1676 the College invested in "a book of the Benefactors," costing £2 4s., together with a "frontispiece of the benefactors' book £2."

The first book-plate of the Library, dated 1703, is rare and of some value to collectors, who would grudge seeing two copies of it in almost every one of the older books. Subsequently a plain engraving of the College arms was used, which was again superseded a year or so ago by a fine large plate, designed by Mr. Muirhead Bone, showing a view of the College from the corner by All Saints'.

The two rather shabby-looking portraits of the Founders hanging in the Senior Library may possibly be those which, in 1670, were bought for £10. The small strong box is also kept here, and dates from about the early sixteenth century.

THE HALL

ALTHOUGH somewhat dark and tending to be a trifle small for modern needs, Lincoln Hall compares most favourably with those of other Colleges. The want of light is due to the fact that two of the windows have been blocked up by the fire-place and the Grove buildings, but its very defects seem to make for a feeling of cosiness and comfort, added to which the room as a whole shows little alteration after so many years. Built in 1437 by John Forrest, it still possesses its original chestnut-timbered roof, which was only brought to light again in 1889 when the then existing plaster ceiling was removed. In 1699 the fire-place was moved from the centre of the Hall to its present position, to which alteration is owed the preservation of an original window and the addition of the above-mentioned ceiling for warmth. At the same time the old mullions of the windows were knocked out and plain sashes inserted, and the wainscoting put up, which was afterwards painted over so thickly that, when it was cleaned, it required many applications of sawdust and potash to remove its nine coats of paint and varnish. In 1891 the work of restoration under the superintendence of Mr. T. Graham Jackson was carried out. The windows were faithfully restored, being exact copies of the original window already mentioned as preserved behind the fire-place, where it remains to this day, and the arms of various benefactors and others inserted in coloured glass after the fashion of the old kind which had existed up to 1641. The chimney-piece was designed by Mr. Jackson. In the top left-hand corner a shield bears the arms of the Deanery of Wells (az. a crosier in bend dexter arg., between two keys endorsed and interlaced in bend sinister or), impaling those of John Forrest (az. eight martlets in an orle or). In the opposite corner are the arms of the See of Durham (az. a cross or between four lions rampant arg.) impaling those of Nathaniel Crewe (az. a lion rampant arg.,

66

THE HALL LOOKING SOUTH

a crescent for difference). Below are the College arms, with the initials of the two Founders on either side. The dogs and brass hood over the fire were specially made, also from Mr. Jackson's designs, by the Keswick School of Metal-workers, but the fire-irons themselves are the original ones and very heavy, the shovel weighing 5½ lb., the poker 6½ lb., and the tongs about 11 lb. There are seventeen portraits on the walls, chiefly of the more recent Rectors, the large one in the middle by the "high table" being that of Lord Keeper Williams, Bishop of Lincoln 1621-42, and the generous donor of the present Chapel, and the one immediately above being that of Dr. Edward Tatham, the twenty-sixth Rector.

FIRE-DOG IN HALL

Before the days of Senior and Junior Common Rooms the Hall was the general meeting-place both for Fellows and Undergraduates. Prior to the Civil War one form of amusement was singing carols, and another was to compel the "freshmen" to provide sport by getting on a bench there to "speak some pretty apophthegm, or make a jest or bull, or speak some elegant nonsense to make the company laugh." If they "came off dull," and it must have been hard work to be witty in so cold-blooded a manner, their chins were "tucked," i.e., scratched by a Senior's thumb-nail, and a mouthful of salted ale had to be swallowed. In the sixteenth and seventeenth centuries dinner was served in the Hall at eleven o'clock, but it gradually became later and later, and by the nineteenth had been changed to four in summer and five in winter, till it is now at seven o'clock. This Hall is unique in always having been lighted during dinner by candles only, and this is still the custom, the electric light, installed some five years ago, being only used on special occasions.

Opposite the Hall is the Buttery, combined with the

THE HALL LOOKING NORTH

STONE PILLAR IN
CELLAR

Common Room, and presided over by the "Manciple," where the plate is kept, and whence are served the "commons" of butter and bread, together with wines and groceries of every description. Here may be seen three more of the old chairs such as are in use for the "high table" in Hall, and also a fine table formed of a solid slab of Cornish marble, about 6 ft. 6 in. long, 2 ft. wide, and 2¼ in. thick, the latter the gift of Dr. Edward Treffry, of Fowey, a former member of the College. Underneath the screen and passage-way between the Buttery and the Hall are to be seen three circular pillars with early Norman bases, of one of which an illustration is given. In another cellar, called the Undergraduates' Wine Cellar, further west,

are two square pillars with bases and caps of the same period as the others, while in several places in the walls may be noticed worked stones belonging either to capitals or window arches. Hitherto it has generally been considered that these pillars are, as forming part of the crypt, all that remains of the Church of St. Mildred, though by

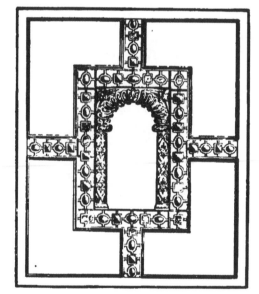

OVERMANTEL IN THE BUTTERY

the most recent authoritative opinion it is thought that the pillars are not as originally built, but have been made up from the old material to hand at a later date, thereby rendering it by no means certain that they occupy their original position, and throwing a doubt upon the theory of the crypt. On the other hand, no very definite explanation has yet been offered, and so an interesting problem still remains to be solved. In 1660 a lock and two keys were bought " for the cloyster," as this part was then called, and for the following year the College Register has a rule " That

no undergraduate Commoner come into the Cloister or cellar." Further along under the Hall is another large cellar excavated in 1640, where the College wine is laid down. The Buttery is joined to the Kitchen by an ancient and narrow building. On the ground floor is the room where the Buttery accounts are kept, containing a nice Jacobean overmantel and the Manciple's candlestick. Above is the Guest Room for visitors, divided as usual into bedroom and sitting-room. This was formerly reached through what was once the Junior Library, but

MANCIPLE'S
CANDLESTICK

when the alterations were made in 1906-7, the Library was turned into the Junior Common Room, and an outside stone staircase was added to give direct access to the Guest Room.

The drawing below is of carved wood, and is fixed up on the wall at the back of the screen. What its history may be, or even what it exactly represents, does not seem quite clear. It is about 7 ft. long and 2 ft. high.

CARVED WOODEN ARMS IN HALL

THE College has no very early pieces of plate, for the collection has been seriously depleted on more than one occasion. In 1640, 75½ oz. 4 dwt. (including "our little old salt") were sold, realizing a sum of £18 4s., in order to help pay for the excavation of the Great Cellar under the Hall. Again, in 1643, Lincoln gave 47 lb. 2 oz. 5 dwt., to Charles I; and finally, in 1756, 450 oz. of old plate were sold to bring in £113, the expenses of obtaining a licence in mortmain. The pieces shown opposite are : (1) Chalice and Paten, silver gilt, London, 1625. Maker, T. H., with a quatrefoil (? cinquefoil) below in a shaped shield. Weight of chalice, 11 oz. 17 dwt. ; of paten, 3 oz. 3 dwt. Diameter of paten, 4⅛ in. ; total height, 9 in. (2) Chapel Candlestick, one of a pair, silver. London, 1683. Maker D. B., between a rayed circle above and a crescent inverted below. Weight, 23 oz. 11 dwt., given by Sir George Wheler as a thank-offering on return from travel abroad. (3) Plain Jug, with unusually long spout, silver. London, 1743. Maker, R^T_CG. Weight, 38 oz. 4 dwt. ; height, 9 in. Arms of donor, Thos. Bathurst, of Lidney, Glos ([sa.] two bars [erm.], in chief three crosses-patées [or]). (4) Grace Cup, silver. London, 1762. Maker, T^C_WW in a circle. Weight, 59 oz. ; height, with cover, 13¼ in. Arms of donor, Sir Peter Davis, of Somerset ([sa.] a cinquefoil [or] between three bugle horns [arg.] stringed [of the second]). (5) Cake Basket, silver. London, 1763 or 1765. Maker illegible. Height, 4½ in. ; diameter, 15¾ by 13¼ in. Arms of donor, Nicholas Corsellis, of Wivenhoe, Essex ([az.] a griffin segreant [or]), quartered with those of Child, of Woodford ([vert] two bars engrailed between three leopards' heads [or]). (6) Flat-topped Communion Flagon, silver gilt. London, 1671. Maker, T. K., with quatrefoil below in a plain shield. Weight, 60 oz. 5 dwt. ; height, 12 in. Arms of donor, Sir Edmund Denton, of Hilsdon, Bucks (arg. two bars [az. should be gu.], in chief three cinquefoils [sa.]. Crest, a lion passant [should be couchant] [or]).

COLLEGE PLATE

COLLEGE PLATE

The pieces here shown are : (7) Jug, silver. London, 1723. Maker, Edward Pocock. Weight, 55 oz. ; height, 12 in. Arms of donor, Henry Hamilton, son of the Archdeacon of Rapho. (Quarterly 1st and 4th [gu.] three cinquefoils [arg.] (? ermine) Hamilton, 2nd and 3rd [arg.] a shakefork [sa.]. Cunningham.) (8) Tankard or sconce, silver. London, 1702. Maker, Rob. Timbull. Weight, 40 oz. 8 dwt. ; height, 7½ in. Arms of donor, Nicholas Corsellis (? father of Nicholas above mentioned). (Quarterly (i) those of Corsellis; (ii) [or] a boar's head in bend [sa.]; (iii) [arg.] three chevrons [az.]; (iv) [gu.] a battle-axe erect [arg.]). (9) Porringer, silver. London, 1680. Maker, I. H., above pellets and a fleur-de-lys. Height, 6¼ in. ; weight, 67 oz. 8 dwt. Arms of donor, Sir Wm. Ellys, Bart. ([gu.] on a fess [arg.] between three crescents [or] as many escallopes [az.] with the Ulster Badge). (10) Soup tureen, silver. London, 1806. Maker, J. E., in a lobe-shaped shield. Height with cover, 10¾ in. ; diameter at mouth, 13⅝ × 9¼ in. An exchange for five old pieces. It is considered to be amongst the best examples of plate in Oxford. (11) Branched Candlestick, Sheffield plate, with lead or pewter embossed ornamentation. Height 19½ in. ; width, 15 in. One of those used in Hall during dinner. (12) Punch-bowl, silver. London, 1726. Maker, F. G., above a mullet in a shield. Height, 7⅞ in. ; diameter at mouth, 11¼ in. Arms of donor, John Medley ([arg.] two bars in chief three mullets [gu.]).

The College possesses another porringer, almost identical with (9), bearing the London mark for 1679 and the arms of the donor, Sir Henry Wright, of Dagenham, Essex. Also a silver-gilt paten, with London mark for 1625 and very clear maker's mark, R. S. and a heart below, all in a plain shield. It has an engraved border, and weighs 10 oz. 4 dwt.

The author is indebted for some of these descriptions to Mr. Moffat's "Oxford Plate," and for the heraldry to the Herald's College and the Rev. H. L. Elliot, of Gosfield, Essex.

COLLEGE PLATE

NATHANIEL CREWE

IN 1652 there entered Lincoln one who was destined to be its greatest benefactor. Nathaniel Crewe was son of the wealthy John Crewe, afterwards Baron Crewe, of Stene, in Northamptonshire. In 1656 he was made a Fellow, and four years later took an active part in the Restoration. As already mentioned, Crewe made a favourable impression upon Charles II when he visited Oxford, and the result was seen in 1666 when he became a Chaplain in ordinary to the King. From that time he attended regularly at Court, and in 1671 was made Bishop of Oxford, being translated three years later to the See of Durham. On the death of his father he succeeded to the Barony, and was thus the first nobleman to unite in one person both temporal and spiritual peerages.

Crewe's benefactions to the College of which he was so fond were not confined to many and generous gifts of money. As a scholar he brought about a keener appreciation of true scholarship, as Sub-Rector his firmness and strong discipline made wholesome changes in College manners and morals, as Rector he showed himself a wise governor and sound financier, and as a courtier and a gentleman he loved to exercise an open-handed hospitality such as his wealth so easily permitted.

THE RIGHT REV. NATHANIEL CREWE, D.D.,
LORD BISHOP OF DURHAM

THE KITCHEN AND SOCIAL GRADES

WHETHER the Kitchen as existing to-day is the actual Winton or Winchester Hall, bought from St. Frideswyde's in 1439, is not definitely known, but it certainly is the oldest building in the College. This view shows the pump and its Penthouse, together with the entrance to the Kitchen which, though small, is 37 feet in height. On the left is the Guest Room, with its outside staircase added in 1907, near which is a good leaden cistern (1745), recently discovered behind one of the houses in Turl Street. The College accounts are, of course, full of references to culinary matters. In 1487 a "grydern" (gridiron) was bought "pro coquina," and a dozen "trenchars." In 1508 "to Carter mendyng the synk before the kecyn, 2d." There was also a "poudryng barell for powdered bef" (i.e., salted beef), "pannes of aerth to put fyshe in in Lent," and "knyves for the cooke to choppe herbes withe-all." The spits which, up till a year or so ago, were used for cooking on "gaudies" or other festive occasions, had to be mended in 1561, and the "smyth" required "48 pounde of yron and a halfe to make two spytts." A salt "cubord" was a necessity in the days of strict observance of Lent, and was therefore duly provided. Then again coal was required, and in 1642 the Bursar discovered that the colliers had been cheating the College over the charcoal, and considered that he verified the saying, "Dixit Diabolus 'carbonario omne nigrum' (With the collier everything is black)"! A few years later "sea-cole"

78

THE KITCHEN EXTERIOR

(i.e., pit coal brought by sea from Newcastle) was used instead as being cheaper, and about the same time 11s. 8d. was spent on "making the Penthouse new at the kitchin hatch." There seems to have been a fair variety of food. Friends gave "venesone," and College tenants either brought their rent in kind, or sent presents of hens, apples, capons, a "gammon of bakone," and other eatables. A common dish used to be "brawne," which was tied up in canvas and seethed in "peny ale," while Lent was the time for salted fish and oysters, which were bought in large quantities. Besides this the

LEADEN CISTERN (1745)

College in the sixteenth century had its own "appyll hows" (apple house) and "pyegyn" (pigeon) or "dauve" house, whence came the materials for mighty "pegyn pastres," and apparently also swans, which were marked by the town swanherd and kept with those belonging to the City.

A brief notice of some of the social grades in the College, besides those already mentioned, may not be out of place here. Fellow or Gentlemen-Commoners, the sons of knights, are first found in 1606. They paid larger fees, and were socially on a level with the Fellows, being accorded the prefix of "Mr." They were not subject to College routine, and had certain privileges, e.g., "not to go bow before the Fellows as other commoners do," and "to sit at the Fellows' table 'till they are a mess of themselves,'" and when there were four admitted they had their own table, but were obliged to rise at dinner and supper as soon as the Fellows' grace-cup was brought in. For these privileges, on coming "up," they had to present a piece

THE KITCHEN INTERIOR

of plate to the College value £10, the private use of which they were allowed while in residence. It is from this source that a large part of the present plate is derived. B.A. Commoners were B.A.'s who remained "up" till they took their M.A., some being even resident in College. The "Scholars of the House" were four in number, elected on the Joan Traps' benefaction, and so called to distinguish them from the "Servitors," a poor class of students who waited upon the Fellows in return for their keep and education. The Servitors again were subdivided into "batlers" and "poor scholars," the former a slightly higher grade; but none lost any social status because of their menial services—in fact, many took their degrees and were eligible for Fellowships. There were also, of course, the ordinary Undergraduate Commoners, sons of private gentlemen, such as form the bulk of the College to-day. In the seventeenth century the usual age for matriculation was from fifteen to eighteen, though two cases are known as early as thirteen. Then followed the general servants. In 1521 these were the cook (cocus), the barber (barbitonsor), and Elizabeth Kirke the laundress (lotrix), together with the manciple (mancipium), and the butler (promus). The two last were kept as distinct offices up to quite recent times, but are now united under the present Manciple, Mr. Lewis. As a regular official the porter was not appointed till 1670, previous to which date his duties were discharged by one of the Scholars, or perhaps by the "pauperculus," who is mentioned occasionally, but whose functions are not definitely known. As to the former the College Register records in 1660: "Wh^m H^y Rose, a schollar of this College, did formerly officiate as porter and had no allowance for his paynes, the College now forgives him that money w^h usually is demanded of all who take degrees, and the College takes no fee from him for his B.A." These degree fees seem to have been first charged in 1641.

The illustration on the next page shows the Oxford Almanack for 1743, with a view of the College engraved by

THE OXFORD ALMANACK, MDCCXLIII

Vertue. At the top are seen the Founders and various benefactors, such as Bishop Williams holding a drawing of his
Chapel screen, and, presumably, John Forrest, with his Hall in
his hand. On either side of the College are the two Mother
Churches: All Saints on the left, and St. Michael's on the
right, while scattered about are the arms of various persons
connected with Lincoln; and below is the Almanack for the year,
together with the officers of the University.

MISCELLANEA

LINCOLN has one or two interesting customs. The Sub-Rectorship and Bursarship are yearly offices, filled by election on November 6th, one of the two Chapter days. At a meeting held the evening before the two officials resign and the Sub-Rector hands over his whip as the emblem of his office. On this occasion the Manciple provides whisky-punch—formerly it used to be egg-flip—and on the resignation of the Sub-Rector glasses are filled and a toast is drunk, with the words, "Bon repos, Sub-Rector." The same is done in the case of the Bursar, with "Bon repos, Bursar," when it is called "Drowning the Bursar." The whip above mentioned is composed entirely of stout whip-cord, and is a genuine survival of medieval times, when no doubt it was wielded with considerable effect! There is also an exact copy of it in the possession of the Rector.

THE SUB-
RECTOR'S
WHIP

Another custom is the method of ringing the bell for Chapel. It is first rung steadily for about three minutes, changing towards the end to short, quick strokes; there is then a pause for one minute, and finally it is struck for the number of the days of the month. It is easy to see that the beginning of the month usually means that some are late for morning Chapel owing to the fewness of the strokes, whereas towards the end it is much easier to be in time. This idea of a bell almanac is occasionally met elsewhere, but when it first originated is unknown.

THE REV. MARK PATTISON, B.D.

MISCELLANEA

THE system of "sconcing" is a very general Oxford custom, but is not kept up to the extent that it used to be. It is a penalty imposed by the head of the table upon anyone who, during Hall time, is guilty of swearing, punning, quoting three words of Latin or four of Scripture, appearing in a light coat or trousers, or breaking similar rules. The offender is "sconced" at the Buttery in two quarts of any liquor he may like to choose, which are brought in the tankard already shown amongst the College Plate. It is first presented to the culprit to drink, and is then passed round the table, beginning at the head, until it is finished. A further rule is that the drinker must hold the tankard by one hand only. The person sconced is allowed the first taste, to give him the chance of "flooring" the sconce, i.e., drinking the whole quantity off at one draught if he can, and it is reported to have been done, when he is entitled to sconce the person who imposed it. Any appeal against the sconce is to the Senior Scholar in Hall, and from him to the High Table.

The call for grace at "Hall" is made by the Senior Fellow present striking the table with a wooden trencher, which has survived from earlier days. The Grace itself is recited by the Senior Scholar among the Freshmen who may be present.

What are known as the "Gaudies" are particular occasions of festivity, with a special dinner in Hall. Formerly they were held on the anniversaries of certain benefactors' deaths and feasts of the Church, but in modern times they are confined to two, the Senior Gaudy for the Fellows on All Saints' Day and the Junior Gaudy for the undergraduates, but on no particular date.

MISCELLANEA

EVERY undergraduate must "keep" twelve terms in residence before he may take his degree, and the means of keeping them varies with the Colleges. In Lincoln it is necessary that a "commons" of bread should be taken out from the Buttery every day during term, though, of course, failure to comply with this regulation never occurs, but non-attendance at forty chapels during term, or any serious misdemeanour, may lead to the same penalty being imposed, namely, that the term will not be allowed to count.

There are two literary societies in the College, the "Davenant," named after the Poet Laureate, and the "Fleming"; while the "Goblins," named after the "Imp," is the College dining club. The two last are twentieth century foundations.

Following the portrait of so brilliant a scholar as Mark Pattison is a fitting place to mention a few of Lincoln's other well-known sons of recent years. Among these are : the Rev. Dr. William Ince, Reg. Prof. of Divinity (Hutchins Scholar 1842), Sir William Ramsay (Fellow 1885); Prof. A. J. Church, of London University (Scholar 1847); Prof. W. J. Ashley, of Harvard University (Fellow 1885); Sir Alfred Hopkinson, Principal of Owens College (Scholar 1869); the late Rev. G. C. Bell, formerly Headmaster of Marlborough (Scholar 1851); Rev. H. A. James, Headmaster of Rugby (Scholar 1864); the late Lord Justice Cave; Prof. W. Baldwin Spencer, of Melbourne University (Fellow 1886), and many others of high attainments with whom Lincoln is proud to be connected.

THE GROVE was originally Olifant Hall, bought in 1463 from University College, and was known as the "Cooke's Garden." In 1606 the Rector was allowed to have it for his private use, provided he supplied "sufficient wholesome and sweet herbes" for College use when necessary. In 1739 there was "a building behind the College Hall, consisting of six chambers for the Commoners," wainscoted and hung with Kidderminster hangings. These rooms were replaced in 1880 by the present building from the design of Mr. T. Graham Jackson, bearing Crewe's motto, "Vis unita fortior."

On Ascension Day it is generally the custom to go round and beat the bounds of the parishes of St. Michael's and All Saints' together, though it is not always done regularly every year. The illustration shows the Rev. W. Mansell Merry, Vicar of St. Michael's, with the boys and men of the choirs and the churchwardens on their way through Lincoln, and by a small door, specially unlocked for the occasion, into Brasenose College. Their labours ended, the beaters are regaled in Hall with luncheon of a homely character, together with ground-ivy ale. This remarkably nasty concoction, formerly called gil or gell-ale, is beer in which ground-ivy has been steeped for twenty-four hours previously. It is also usual to throw pennies into the quadrangle to be scrambled for by the youthful members among the beaters. The history of this entertainment appears to have no more definite authority than that of custom, but that it has been in existence for some long time is shown by a reference to it in 1604 in the College Account Books. For some years past also B.N.C. men have been accustomed to come through and claim a drink of the ale, though whether they have a definite right to do so is not certain. It is thought that possibly in theory all the parishioners may have a claim, in which case no doubt Brasenose men would be included.

THE GROVE

BEATING THE BOUNDS

LOGGAN'S VIEW

IN 1675 the College paid thirty shillings "to Mr. Loggan for his buke," which he brought out about the University at the request of Dr. Fell, Bishop of Oxford and Dean of Christ Church, who was anxious to advertise the University throughout Europe. On the opposite page is his bird's-eye view of the College, drawn for his book, and beneath it an attempt at reconstruction, to show the differences between his day and modern times. Notice the dog in the quadrangle in Loggan's plan, which would now be a terrible breach of College rules.

The following are just a few interesting entries gathered from the College account books. (1521) "For threyd to make a net for taking the chowghys (i.e., choughs or birds generally) abowte the College." (1550) "To ye mendyng of ye Dyvynytye Schole 40^d." (1575) "For carriinge from Botlie our borde by water 8^d, by lande from fryer bacon's studye at 2 loades 12^d."; the wood, very largely elm, came by river to Folly Bridge, probably the "hyebridge" or highbridge mentioned in these accounts, where the College owned property which has now been sold. The allusion to Bacon, who lived over the gateway on the bridge, is interesting: (1595) "To the poore at Portmeadow," this was the common property of the city before the Domesday Survey. (1613) "The overplus of that which was receyved and payed for the Lady Elizabeth's ayde 5^s 4^d"; that is, the "aid" levied on the marriage of James I's daughter with the Elector Palatine at a time when James was particularly in want of money. (1618) "For glasse in Slad's, Devonant, and Ford's studdie, 13^d"; this is most probably a reference to Sir William Davenant. (1673) "To the Almsmen of Bartholomews, 2^s"; that is the hospital belonging to Oriel College, of which the Chapel still remains, close to our Athletic Ground.

THE BARGE AND PAVILION

COLLEGE rowing and games have always been rather handicapped owing to the small number of men in residence, but Lincoln has no reason to be ashamed of her record. In the "Torpids" the boat made seven bumps in 1882 and 1901, and six in 1904. The rudder of the "Eight" is still preserved which in 1867 started tenth and finished fifth, and which by going up to fourth place the following year reached the highest position to which the Lincoln boat has ever attained. In 1896 and 1903-4-5-6 successively, the College won the Clinker Fours, but after the last occasion the race was abolished, and the cup so worthily earned by Lincoln was taken for other purposes. The present Barge, which dates from 1901, is in one of the best positions on the river, being so well placed that spectators can watch the course of the races from the Long Bridges to the winning post.

The Athletic Ground at the top of the Cowley Road, containing about six acres, was acquired in 1903, and together with the Pavilion answers the purposes of every game. There is no room here to name the many "Blues" who have upheld the honour of their College and University. In 1874 there were five in College, three athletic, one Rugby, and one for rowing. The latter was the present Fellow and Law Tutor, Dr. James Williams, who rowed five in the 'Varsity boat, and yet found time to take a First Class in both "Mods." and "Greats." He thus holds the record of being the only rowing "Blue" who has ever been a Fellow of Lincoln. In later years an Exhibitioner, F. A. Leslie-Jones, made his name a household word in Rugby football, and many others in every branch of sport have continued to keep up the reputation of the College, and show that Lincoln in proportion to its size is by no means behind its rivals in this respect. The carved shields of the College arms, both on the Barge and Pavilion, were the generous gift of the Rector.

THE BARGE

THE PAVILION

ALL SAINTS' CHURCH

REFERENCE has already been made to All Saints' Church, which, with its chantry of St. Anne, is one of the Mother Churches of the College. The tower is seen in the illustration opposite. In 1521 two city Guilds, those of the glovers (cirothecariorum) and the skinners (pellipariorum), used to celebrate their special Masses here, and four years later the account books acknowledge a quaint receipt of 8d. from the Churchwardens for a swarm of bees found in the churchyard. The spire of the old Church fell down in 1700, demolishing the roof in its descent, and designs for the new building were at once supplied by Henry Aldrich, Dean of Christ Church, subscriptions being given from all quarters, and not least by Nathaniel Crewe, who gave more than £300 altogether. The interior is an oblong, with no aisles or chancel proper, and shows a large span of roof with good plastered ceiling, pilasters with very finely carved capitals, and the arms of all the subscribers, including Queen Anne, round the building. Here are the tombs of several Rectors, including Hutchins and Tatham, as well as Fellows and others connected with Lincoln. After the election of a new Rector for the College the ceremony of his installation always takes place in this Church.

When St. Martin's or Old Carfax Church was done away with some years ago, it was incorporated with All Saints', to which its fine font was removed.

THE COLLEGE LOOKING
TOWARDS ALL SAINTS' CHURCH

ST. MICHAEL'S CHURCH

ST. MICHAEL'S CHURCH "ad portam borealem" provides more of interest than her sister All Saints'. The ancient tower, which once formed part of the city wall, is thought to date possibly from the close of the eleventh century, and would seem to have served for both military and ecclesiastical purposes. The Church itself is of later date, the chancel being early thirteenth century, and the remainder made up of what were originally chantries added in 1260, 1342, and 1524 by various persons. The quaint piece of stone carving, here reproduced, appears to be a portion of a tomb, thought to be connected with a brass near by, dated 1618, to one Gregory Martin, of Exeter College. Being somewhat worn, it gives a good opportunity for speculation as to what may be the various objects represented. The College accounts show that in the early sixteenth century Brasenose (or as they have it, "Brasynnoose") used to give Christmas offerings to St. Michael's and similarly Exeter on the feast of St. Thomas the Martyr, while both Colleges did so at Easter.

STONE CARVING IN ST. MICHAEL'S CHURCH

ST. MICHAEL'S CHURCH : THE TOWER

THE chief source of revenue of these Churches in common with others at Oxford in early times seems to have been the custom of "Sunday pence." This was the sum of one penny per week levied on every house in the parish over the value of twenty shillings per annum, which sum was doubled at the great Festivals of Christmas, Easter, Ascension, and Whitsuntide. In 1525 one William Potycarye, alias Clerke, of All Saints' parish, refused payment, whereupon the College in a test case had him compelled to pay under penalty "of the greater excommunication." In St. Michael's parish to-day there are still some tenements paying quit rents of 4s. 8d. to the Church, which are the survivals of the old "Sunday pence."

Among other property of the College not already mentioned should be noted the "Maiden's Head Hotel" in Turl Street. In 1521 it was apparently called "Swanburn's howse," and was originally granted to All Saints' parish to provide money for repair of the Church. This was subject to certain conditions under which, if they were not fulfilled, it should vest in the College absolutely. In 1577 it is referred to in the account books as "the Maydenhead," but by 1654 it had become the "Globe." In the latter year the College went to law over the title to the inn, perhaps because of some breach of the conditions, lost the case, and found great difficulty in paying the costs. It is now leased by the College to the Feoffees of All Saints' parish for forty years at the nominal rent of 13s. 4d. per annum.

The property, formerly the "Ram Inn," now Nos. 113 and 114 High Street, was in 1436 given to the College by Emelina Carr, Widow. In 1512 rent was received "de domo Johis Skynnar vocat le Ram cum quadam schoppa ei adjunct: £3 11s. 4d." In the middle of the seventeenth century one Peter Sthael, a German professor, was brought over, and had his lecture-room on these premises, which he used to form a club for the study of chemistry. Among his pupils were the famous John Locke,

COLLEGE PROPERTY

whom Anthony Wood calls "a man of a turbulent spirit, clamorous and never contented," and two Lincoln men, Nathaniel Crewe and Robert Wood.

A few names occur in our Bidding Prayer which have hitherto not been mentioned, but which deserve an explanation for their inclusion. Cardinal Beaufort's executors in 1447 were induced by Beke, the Rector, to give 100 marcs to the College out of the money left by him for pious uses; John Bucktot bequeathed, in 1542, his manor of Little Pollicot, in Bucks; John Crosby gave 100 marcs to provide a Fellow who should pray for the benefactor and study the Canon Law, this differed from the other Fellowships in that the holder was not required to proceed to the degree of B.D.; Walter Bate gave (inter alia) a house in the lane north of All Saints' Church, where now is the Fellows' Garden; John Randall in 1622 bequeathed "Ship Hall" in St. Mary Hall Lane, i.e., the old house at the corner by Oriel College, to whom it has since been sold; Sir John Thorold resigned his Fellowship in 1725 on becoming heir to a baronetcy, and afterwards gave £100 to increase the salary of the Bible-clerk; Elizabeth Tatham, the widow of the Rector Edward Tatham, founded a scholarship in his memory; Henry Usher Matthews bequeathed over £2,000 "for the foundationship of an open Scholarship, tenable for three years"; and Edward Wm. Stillingfleet was the founder in 1867 of the reading prize already mentioned.

The "Mitre Hotel," a famous piece of College property, has already been referred to in the Introduction. About the middle of the seventeenth century it was commonly reported that Mass was still celebrated in the University, the allusion being to this inn, the lessees of which were for many years noted Roman Catholics. The accounts have a mention in 1653 of arrears of rent from Widow Davis "pro Mitrâ hospitio."

IFFLEY MILL

IN 1444 William Finderne, of Childrey, gave land and money to the College, and with the latter was bought, among other property, the famous mill. It has been suggested that the mill mentioned in Domesday as being "below" the city may well be that at Iffley, and at any rate the College deeds relating to it date back to 1285, thus showing a clear record of continuous work for more than six hundred years. In 1487 the rent was £5 and repairs numerous, and in the same year was paid "for a spyndell of yren (iron) pro molendino de Yeftley (Iffley) 3s. 3d." This "wheyll spyndyll of the myll" had to be mended by "the smyth att the est gaytt" (i.e., at the bottom of the High Street) a few years later, and in 1529 "Caxston carpentar" made "the flowde gatts abowte the looke (lock), fyndyng all maner of stuffe" for 2s. 2d. !

During the sixteenth century it seems to have been the custom for the Fellows every year to have a "fishyng daye" at Iffley, winding up with a jollification afterwards. Apparently, however, the tenant found it was too much of a nuisance, for later on he used to pay the Fellows to give up their outing.

The tenant of the mill has the right to exact and keep for himself a toll of one halfpenny per person crossing the sluices.

On the night of May 20, 1908, the old mill caught fire from some unknown cause, and was completely burnt down. Whether it is to be rebuilt and restored to its original use or not is for others to decide, but at any rate for the present a long and useful career has come to an untimely end, whilst lovers of the picturesque must ever regret the loss for all time of one of the most charming pictures on the River Thames.

IFFLEY MILL

RICHARD FLEMING (BISHOP OF LINCOLN, 1420-1431)	THOMAS ROTHERAM (BISHOP OF LINCOLN, 1471-1480)	WILLIAM CHAMBERLEYN (1429—1434)
JOHN BEKE (1434—1451)	JOHN TRISTROPP (1451—1479)	GEORGE STRANGWAYS (1480—1488)
WILLIAM BETHOME (1488—1493)	THOMAS BANK (1493—1505)	THOMAS DRAX (1505—1519)
JOHN COTTISFORD (1519—1539)	HUGH WESTON (1539—1556)	CHRISTOPHER HARGREAVES (1556—1558)
HENRY HENSHAW (1558—1560)	FRANCIS BABINGTON (1560—1563)	JOHN BRIDGEWATER (1563—1574)
JOHN TATHAM (1574—1576)	JOHN UNDERHILL (1577—1590)	RICHARD KILBY (1590—1620)
PAUL HOOD (1622—1668)	NATHANIEL CREWE (1668—1672)	NATHANIEL CREWE (1668—1672)
THOMAS MARSHALL (1672—1685)	FITZHERBERT ADAMS (1685—1719)	JOHN MORLEY (1719—1731)
EUSEBY ISHAM (1731—1755)	RICHARD HUTCHINS (1755—1781)	CHARLES MORTIMER (1781—1784)
JOHN HORNER (1784—1794)	EDWARD TATHAM (1792—1834)	JOHN RADFORD (1834—1851)
JAMES THOMPSON (1851—1860)	MARK PATTISON (1861—1884)	WILLIAM WALTER MERRY (1884—)

THE COLLEGE GRACE

BENIGNISSIME Pater qui providentiâ tuâ regis, liberalitate pascis et benedictione conservas omnia quae creaveris, benedicas nobis te quaesumus et hisce creaturis in usum nostrum ut illae sanctificatae sint et nobis salutares et ut nos inde corroborati magis apti reddamur ad omnia opera bona in laudem tui nominis aeterni per Jesum Christum Dominum Nostrum. Amen.

ENVOI

Mater ave atque vale!
  Now that it is all too late
Reverence increaseth daily,
  Reverence inadequate.

Three short years ago the starting,
  Race for good or evil won,
Three short years, and now the parting;
  Hath the race been lost or won?

Ah, that I have never known thee,
  Alma Mater, till the end!
Wiser now I wax and own thee
  Mother, teacher, lover, friend.

Deeper evermore and deeper
  Sinks remembrance of thy halls,
Where the red Virginia creeper
  Fades in flame along the walls.

Where the curfew music, spreading
  Mist-like over stream and town,
Tells the hour to shepherds treading
  Homeward on the folded down.

We thy children, Alma Mater,
  Fail in words of love and fire,
History may tell thee later
  What a mother can inspire.

James Williams.

INDEX

* Denotes a Pen-and-Ink Drawing

INDEX

INDEX

INDEX

Lightning Source UK Ltd.
Milton Keynes UK
UKOW06n2245291015

261702UK00006B/88/P